SO-ASL-612

WITHDRAWN

World Book's Documenting History
Aboriginal Rights Movement

WORLD BOOK

a Scott Fetzer company
Chicago

www.worldbookonline.com

World Book, Inc.
233 N. Michigan Avenue
Chicago, IL 60601
U.S.A.

For information about other World Book publications, visit our website at **http://www.worldbookonline.com** or call **1-800-WORLDBK (967-5325).**

For information about sales to schools and libraries, call **1-800-975-3250 (United States),** or **1-800-837-5365 (Canada).**

© 2011 World Book, Inc. All rights reserved. This volume may not be reproduced in whole or in part in any form without prior written permission from the publisher.

WORLD BOOK and the GLOBE DEVICE are registered trademarks or trademarks of World Book, Inc.

Library of Congress Cataloging-in-Publication Data

Aboriginal rights movement.
    p. cm. -- (World Book's documenting history)
  Includes bibliographical references and index.
  Summary: "A history of the Aboriginal rights movement in Australia, based on primary source documents and other historical artifacts. Features include period art works and photographs; excerpts from literary works, letters, speeches, broadcasts, and diaries; summary boxes; a timeline; maps; and a list of additional resources"-- Provided by publisher.
  ISBN 978-0-7166-1499-9
  1. Aboriginal Australians--Civil rights--Sources--Juvenile literature. 2. Aboriginal Australians--Legal status, laws, etc.--Sources--Juvenile literature. 3. Aboriginal Australians--Government relations--Sources --Juvenile literature. 4. Civil rights movements--Australia--History--Sources--Juvenile literature. 5. Australia--Race relations--History--Sources--Juvenile literature. 6. Australia--Social conditions--Sources --Juvenile literature. I. World Book, Inc.
  DU124.C48A36 2011
  323.119'915--dc22

                  2010024982

World Book's Documenting History
Set ISBN 978-0-7166-1498-2
Printed in Malaysia by TWP Sdn Bhd, JohorBahru
1st printing September 2010

Staff

Executive Committee

Vice President and Chief Financial Officer
  Donald D. Keller
Vice President and Editor in Chief
  Paul A. Kobasa
Vice President, Licensing & Business Development
  Richard Flower
Chief Technology Officer
  Tim Hardy
Managing Director, International
  Benjamin Hinton
Director, Human Resources
  Bev Ecker

Editorial

Associate Director, Supplementary Publications
  Scott Thomas
Editor
  Sara Dreyfuss
Senior Editor
  Kristina Vaicikonis

Manager, Contracts & Compliance
(Rights & Permissions)
  Loranne K. Shields
Manager, Research, Supplementary Publications
  Cheryl Graham
Editorial Researcher
  Jon Wills
Administrative Assistant
  Ethel Matthews

Editorial Administration

Director, Systems and Projects
  Tony Tills
Senior Manager, Publishing Operations
  Timothy Falk
Associate Manager, Publishing Operations
  Audrey Casey

Graphics and Design

Manager
  Tom Evans
Coordinator, Design Development and Production
  Brenda B. Tropinski
Senior Designer
  Isaiah W. Sheppard, Jr.
Associate Designer
  Matt Carrington

Production

Director, Manufacturing and Pre-Press
  Carma Fazio
Manufacturing Manager
  Steven K. Hueppchen
Production/Technology Manager
  Anne Fritzinger
Production Specialist
  Curley Hunter
Proofreader
  Emilie Schrage

Marketing

Associate Director, School and Library Marketing
  Jennifer Parello

Produced for World Book by
Arcturus Publishing Limited

Writer: Joseph Harris
Editors: Patience Coster, Alex Woolf
Designer: Jane Hawkins

Contents

Warning: Aboriginal Australians and Torres Strait Islanders should be aware that this volume includes images and names of people now deceased.

The First Australians

FOR MORE THAN 200 YEARS, AUSTRALIAN ABORIGINES have struggled against domination and bad treatment by white Australians. They have had to fight for even the most basic rights. Yet the ancestors of the Aborigines were the first Australians. They arrived in Australia at least 50,000 years ago, long before Europeans came to the continent. Most scholars believe the Aborigines' ancestors came from Southeast Asia and traveled to Australia in canoes and on rafts. They arrived in the north. Over the next 10,000 to 20,000 years, they moved southward across mainland Australia. They settled in the coastal regions, the tropical rain forests, the deserts, and the nearby islands, including Tasmania and the Torres Strait Islands.

1

You are the New Australians, but we are the Old Australians. We have in our arteries the blood of the Original Australians, who have lived in this land for many thousands of years. You came here only recently, and you took our land away from us by force. You have almost *exterminated* [wiped out] our people. . . .

Jack Patten and William Ferguson, 1938

◀ Two Aboriginal leaders explain why their people, the "Old Australians," have as much right to their country as do white people, the "New Australians." The two leaders, Jack Patten (1905-1957) and William Ferguson (1882-1950), emphasized that the Aborigines were Australia's original inhabitants and lived there thousands of years before white people arrived. These words appeared in "Aborigines Claim Citizen Rights!," a pamphlet published in 1938, the 150th anniversary of white settlement.

2

▶ An Aboriginal rock painting depicts two people and a fish in a traditional style called *X-ray painting*. X-ray painting shows the bones and internal organs of people and animals within the outline of their bodies. The Aborigines made these paintings on rock surfaces, particularly rock walls sheltered by overhangs. Many rock paintings are at least 40,000 years old.

4

3

In 1969, I invited a team of archaeologists and earth scientists to inspect a site in western New South Wales. . . . burnt bones [were] embedded in a carbonate block. . . . On [Welsh-born Australian archaeologist] Rhys Jones [1941-2001] lifting fragments of the carbonate block, out fell an unmistakable piece of human *mandible* [jawbone]! This was not just evidence of human presence; it was the remains of humanity itself. Thus began the saga of Mungo Lady, the cremation site of whom has now been dated to 41,000 years.

Jim Bowler, 2005

▲ In a 2005 article, the Australian geologist James M. (Jim) Bowler (1940?-   ) recalls an exciting discovery he and his team made in 1969. They found the ancient remains of a woman near Lake Mungo, a dry lake bed in New South Wales. In 1974, scientists found male bones in the same area. The two skeletons were nicknamed Mungo Lady and Mungo Man. They are the oldest human remains so far discovered in Australia.

4

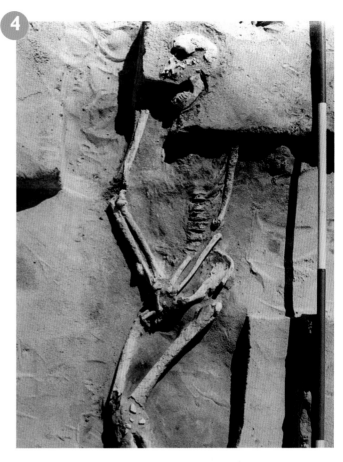

▲ The ancient human remains known as Mungo III or Mungo Man were found near Lake Mungo in 1974. The body was decorated with ocher, a brownish-yellow coloring made from clay. The Australian Aborigines still use ocher in their art. Australian Aboriginal culture is one of the oldest in the world, with customs, rituals, and beliefs dating back tens of thousands of years.

NOW YOU KNOW

- The first Australians were ancestors of present-day Aborigines who arrived on the continent around 50,000 years ago.
- Scholars think the Aborigines traveled from Southeast Asia by sea.
- Aboriginal customs, such as rock painting and decorating with ocher, have survived for tens of thousands of years.

A Sacred Land

FOR THOUSANDS OF YEARS, ABORIGINAL PEOPLES LIVED on the Australian continent, adapting to its different regions and climates. They were hunter-gatherers, traveling great distances to hunt such animals as emus and kangaroos, and to gather plants for food. They fished in rivers, lakes, and the sea. They spread across the country and formed hundreds of *clans* (groups of related families). Aboriginal clans spoke many different languages and lived in their own traditional territories. Ancient Australians believed that they had a spiritual connection to the land that supported them. They believed that people had a duty to take care of the land.

1

Our story is in the land . . . it is written in those sacred places. My children will look after those places, that's the law. Dreaming place . . . you can't change it, no matter who you are. No matter you rich man, no matter you king. You can't change it. My children got to hang onto this story. This important story. I hang onto this story all my life. My father tell me this story.

Bill Neidjie, 1986

◀ In his book *Australia's Kakadu Man* (1986), Bill Neidjie (1913-2002) explains the connection between his people and their land. According to Aboriginal tradition, ancestor spirits shaped the landscape during a magical time called the Dreaming. Neidjie, a member of the Gagudju people of Australia's Northern Territory, helped establish Kakadu National Park on his people's traditional land between 1979 and 1991.

▶ Yami Lester (1949?-), an Aborigine *stockman* (livestock worker), explains in his autobiography *Yami* (1993) that he learned about the Dreaming from his parents, members of the Yankunytjatjara people of South Australia. The Aborigines believe that ancestor spirits created the world during the Dreaming. The spirits traveled across the land, making and naming the places, animals, plants, and people who would belong there. The Aborigines celebrate the Dreaming through art, ceremonies, dance, songs, and stories.

2

[My parents] just talked about the country. And I believed what they said. You couldn't doubt, it was just something real. The country wasn't just hills or creeks or trees. And I didn't feel like it was fairy tales they told me. It was real. Our kuuti, the force that gives us life. Somebody created it, and whoever created it did it for us, so we could live and hunt and have a good time. That's how we come to be here because the *malu* [kangaroo] and *ngintaka* [a type of lizard] created this image for us to live and breathe: the plants, the language, the people.

Yami Lester, 1993

▼ The huge loaf-shaped rock formation known as Uluru is sacred to Aborigines. According to their tradition, Uluru and other sites connect the world to the Dreaming. One story is that Uluru formed after snake spirits fought a bloody battle. The snakes turned to stone and became the rock. The blood they shed colored the rock red. As the sun rises or sets, the rock glows a deep red. For a long time, white Australians ignored the name Uluru and called the site Ayers Rock.

NOW YOU KNOW

- The Australian Aborigines lived off the land by hunting, fishing, and gathering plants.
- According to Aboriginal tradition, ancestor spirits shaped the land during a magical time called the Dreaming.
- The Aborigines have handed down stories about the Dreaming from the distant past.

Strangers Invade

IN 1606, WILLEM JANSZ, A DUTCH SEA CAPTAIN, was the first recorded European to sight Australia. The Dutch saw only harsh parts of the continent and did not establish colonies. In 1770, James Cook, a British naval captain, landed at what would be called Botany Bay on Australia's eastern coast, which has a milder climate. Although Aborigines already lived there, Cook claimed the land for Great Britain (now part of the United Kingdom). He named it New South Wales. In 1788, a group of British ships called the First Fleet reached New South Wales to establish a prison colony. At that time, Great Britain sent some of its convicts to distant prison colonies. The convicts and guards of the First Fleet became the first white settlers in Australia.

▶ In his journal entry for Aug. 22, 1770, Captain James Cook describes how he claimed the southeastern coast of Australia for Britain. Because the Aborigines were not settled farmers, Cook assumed that they did not own the land and that it was open for British settlement. European law viewed any place that was not settled permanently as *terra nullius*, a Latin legal term meaning that it belonged to no one. From the beginning, Europeans denied the Aborigines' right to their ancestral lands.

1 ... *I now once more hoisted English Coleurs [the English flag], and in the Name of His Majesty King George the Third took possession of the whole Eastern Coast ... by the name of New South Wales, together with all the Bays, Harbours Rivers and Islands ...*

James Cook, 1770

▶ The first convicts arrive at Port Jackson, commonly known as Sydney Harbour, in January 1788. To relieve crowding in British prisons, the government used *transportation* (sending convicts to prison colonies overseas). Few convicts in Australia served their full sentences in prison. Instead, most prisoners were forced to work for free settlers, often in bad conditions. However, many convicts eventually built houses and established families, businesses, and farms.

8

3

They [the Aborigines] pointed with their sticks to the best landing place & met us in the most cheerful manner, shouting & dancing. . . . these people mixed with ours & all hands [everyone in the group] danced together.

William Bradley, 1788

◀ William Bradley (1757?-1833), a British naval officer on the First Fleet, describes in his journal how the Aborigines warmly welcomed the newcomers to New South Wales on Jan. 29, 1788. But relations soon became strained, and many Aborigines came to view the Europeans as unwelcome invaders.

▼ An engraving from the early 1800's shows the thriving British settlement at Port Jackson that became the city of Sydney. British settlement expanded rapidly, driving the Aborigines (seen in the foreground) from their traditional lands.

4

NOW YOU KNOW

- A Dutchman, Willem Jansz, was the first European to record sightings of Australia.
- In 1770, Captain James Cook claimed the eastern coast of Australia for Britain.
- In 1788, the First Fleet arrived and founded a British prison colony in New South Wales.

First Encounters

THE FIRST GOVERNOR OF NEW SOUTH WALES, ARTHUR PHILLIP (1738-1814), wanted to befriend the Aborigines. But, like most other Europeans of his time, he assumed that Aborigines were inferior to whites and should be "civilized." To learn about the local Eora people of New South Wales, Governor Phillip kidnapped several of them. The first was a man called Arabanoo (1758?-1789), who soon died of smallpox. Next, Phillip seized Bennelong (1764?-1813) and Colebee (1754?-1797). Bennelong remained with the British the longest. He learned to speak English and to drink alcohol. He drank so much that his health suffered, and he died an alcoholic. His unhappy life suggested that the future would not be easy for Aborigines.

1

. . . they [the Aborigines] certainly rank very low, even in the scale of savages. . . . Though suffering from the *vicissitudes* [changes] of their climate, strangers to clothing, though feeling the sharpness of hunger . . . ignorant of cultivating the earth—a less enlightened state we shall exclaim can hardly exist. . . . But if [we] examine individually the persons who compose the community, they will certainly rise in estimation . . . he who shall make just allowance for *uninstructed nature* [lack of education] will hardly accuse any of those persons [Arabanoo, Bennelong, and Colebee] of stupidity or *deficiency of apprehension* [lack of understanding].

Watkin Tench, 1793

◀ Watkin Tench (1759?-1833), a British officer, describes the Aborigines in his book *A Complete Account of the Settlement at Port Jackson* (1793). He calls them savages because they wore little clothing and did not farm. He and other Europeans failed to realize that the Aborigines had a unique culture and superior survival skills. But Tench admitted the intelligence of some individual Aborigines, including Arabanoo, Bennelong, and Colebee.

2

▶ An engraving from the early 1800's depicts white people trading with Aborigines. Most colonial art from this period shows the Aborigines as primitive and hostile to Europeans.

10

▶ In 1796, Bennelong wrote or dictated this letter to Mr. Phillips, the property manager of Lord Sydney (1732-1800), the British nobleman for whom Sydney, Australia, is named. Bennelong had just returned from a three-year visit to England. There, the English viewed him as a curiosity and paraded him around like an exotic animal. Things were little better when he returned to Australia. His own people no longer accepted him, and the colonists never fully welcomed him as one of them. He was left to beg for charity from white people until his death in 1813.

③ *Sir, I am very well. I hope you are very well. I live at the Governor's. I have every day dinner there. I have not my wife: another black man took her away . . . he spear'd me in the back, but I better now. . . . Not me go to England no more. I am at home now. . . . Sir, hope all are well in England . . . send me you please some Handkerchiefs for Pocket. You please Sir send me some shoes: two pair you please Sir.*
Bennelong, 1796

④ ◀ A 1790's portait of Bennelong of the Eora people shows him dressed like a British gentleman in a coat, ruffled lace shirt, and fancy *waistcoat* (vest). Bennelong ended up a lonely outcast from both Aboriginal and colonial society.

NOW YOU KNOW

- Most of the British settlers saw the Aborigines as a primitive people.
- Even colonists with good intentions, such as Governor Arthur Phillip, assumed the Aborigines should adopt British customs.
- Bennelong, an Aborigine, was forced to learn British ways, but his life ended sadly.

Conflict and Resistance

AS THE NUMBERS OF CONVICTS AND FREE SETTLERS INCREASED, the colonists settled new places and took over more land. They drove the Aborigines from their traditional homes. Some Aborigines resisted, attacking the colonists. Both sides used violence, but many more Aborigines than colonists were killed. The Europeans had better weapons than the Aborigines had. Many Aborigines died of European diseases to which they had no natural resistance. The conflict caused many colonists to hate Aborigines and attack them even after Aboriginal resistance had ended. Mistrust and mistreatment of Aborigines would last a long time.

1

. . . an open war seemed about that time to have commenced between the natives and the settlers. . . . In their attacks they conducted themselves with much *art* [trickery]; but where that failed, they had recourse to force, and on the least appearance of resistance made use of their spears or clubs. . . . Captain Paterson directed a party of the corps [the New South Wales Corps, a British infantry regiment responsible for keeping order in the colony of New South Wales] . . . to destroy as many as they could . . . and, in the hope of striking terror, to erect *gibbets* [gallows] in different places, whereon the bodies of all they might kill were to be hung.

David Collins, 1798

◄ David Collins (1754-1810), a British official, describes clashes between colonists and Aborigines. Collins—who later founded the city of Hobart, Tasmania—wrote about the conflict in his book *An Account of the English Colony in New South Wales* (1798). The Aborigines often resisted white settlement. Such leaders as Pemulwuy (1750?-1802) of the Eora and Windradyne (1800?-1829) of the Wiradjuri fought bravely. But in the long run, the growing numbers, superior weapons, and better organization of the British settlers defeated the Aborigines.

2

One of the largest holders of Sheep in the Colony, maintained at a public meeting at Bathurst, that the best thing that could be done, would be to shoot all the Blacks and *manure* [fertilize] the ground with their *carcasses* [dead bodies], which was all the good they were fit for! It was recommended likewise that the women and children should especially be shot as the most certain method of getting rid of the race. . . . sad was the *havoc* [damage] made upon the tribes at Bathurst.

Lancelot E. Threlkeld, 1824

► Lancelot E. Threlkeld (1788-1859), an English missionary, describes how white settlers in Bathurst, a frontier town near Sydney, called for killing "Blacks" (Aborigines). Threlkeld's account appeared in a memorandum of a public meeting at Bathurst in 1824. In the fall of that year, troops from Bathurst surrounded and shot groups of Wiradjuri men, women, and children. Historians estimate that the troops killed one-third of the Wiradjuri population. Today, trying to wipe out an entire people would be considered the crime of genocide.

▼ A print shows mounted police shooting Aborigines at Slaughter-house Creek in New South Wales in January 1838. In this attack, the police killed between 60 and 300 of the Kamilaroi people, who were armed only with spears. The British author and artist Godfrey Charles Mundy (1804-1860) created this print, "Mounted Police and Blacks," to illustrate his book *Our Antipodes* (1852).

NOW YOU KNOW

- White settlement increasingly drove the Aborigines from their lands.
- Both sides used violence, but many more Aborigines than colonists died in the fighting.
- White colonists sometimes massacred large numbers of Aborigines.

Betrayal in Tasmania

I N 1803, THE BRITISH SET UP A PRISON COLONY ON THE ISLAND OF TASMANIA, south of mainland Australia. Free settlers arrived in 1804. Warfare soon erupted between the settlers and Tasmanian Aborigines. The Aborigines suffered terrible losses. George Augustus Robinson (1791-1866), a British missionary, persuaded about 200 of the survivors to leave. An Aboriginal woman, Truganini (1812-1876), helped Robinson take her people to Flinders Island in Bass Strait. Colonial officials promised to give them food, clothing, and shelter, and to let them maintain their traditional ways. Instead, missionaries tried to force them to convert to Christianity. Disease, hunger, and homesickness led to the deaths of about 150 of the people by 1842.

▶ An article in a Hobart newspaper on Dec. 1, 1826, argues that the Aborigines should be forced to leave the Tasmanian mainland. George Augustus Robinson tried to save the last Tasmanian Aborigines by persuading them to leave their land. From 1829 to 1834, he collected about 200 survivors from the mainland and took them under his care to Flinders Island off northern Tasmania.

1

THE GOVERNMENT MUST REMOVE THE NATIVES—IF NOT, THEY WILL BE HUNTED DOWN LIKE WILD BEASTS AND DESTROYED! . . . We would recommend their being taken, which could easily be effected— placed at King's Island [off northwestern Tasmania] with a small guard of soldiers to protect them, and let them be compelled to grow potatoes, wheat, & catch seals and fish, and by degrees, they will lose their *roving disposition* [wandering habits], and acquire some slight habits of *industry* [steady effort], which is the first step of civilization . . . . If they are sent to King's Island, they will be under restraint, but they will be free from committing, or receiving, violence . . .

Colonial Times, 1826

2

◀ A portrait of Tasmanian Aboriginal leader Truganini by Benjamin Duterrau (1767-1851). Duterrau, who emigrated to Tasmania from England, painted the portrait in around 1835, soon after Truganini had led her people to Flinders Island. She lived long enough—until 1876—to see all of her people die there in miserable conditions.

14

3

Your Petitioners humbly tell Y. M. [Your Majesty] that when we left our own place we were plenty of People, we are now but a little one. . . . Our houses were let fall down & they were never cleaned but were covered with vermin. . . . We were often without Clothes. . . . Dr Jeanneret did not care to mind us when we were sick until we were very bad. Eleven of us died when he was here. He put many of us into Jail for talking to him because we would not be his slaves. He kept from us our Rations when he pleased. . . . We humbly pray Your Majesty the Queen will hear our prayer . . .

Tasmanian Aborigines
of Flinders Island, 1846

◀ A petition from the Tasmanian Aborigines of Flinders Island to Queen Victoria of the United Kingdom describes the miserable conditions on the island. Colonial authorities did not honor their promise that the Aborigines would have a good life. The officials put in charge of them, such as the Flinders Island commandant Henry Jeanneret (1802-1886), a British dentist, treated the Aborigines cruelly and neglected them.

▶ In 1899, Fanny Cochrane Smith (1834-1905) records traditional songs of the Tasmanian Aborigines, which she learned as a child on Flinders Island. Assisting her is Horace Watson of the Royal Society of Tasmania, a scientific organization. Smith's are the only existing recordings of the Tasmanian language.

4

NOW YOU KNOW

- In the early 1800's, violence broke out between white settlers and Tasmanian Aborigines.
- Between 1829 and 1834, the government sent the few remaining Tasmanian Aborigines to live on Flinders Island.
- Colonial officials mistreated the Aborigines on Flinders Island, and their community died out.

Harsh Laws

BY THE MID-1800'S, THE ABORIGINAL POPULATION HAD DECLINED STEEPLY as a result of starvation, disease, and conflict. Australia consisted of a number of separate, British-ruled colonies, each able to make its own laws. In 1869, the colony of Victoria passed an Aboriginal Protection Act that was supposed to help Aborigines by providing for their needs. The act set up a Board for the Protection of Aborigines with the power to control Aborigines' lives. The board regulated where they lived and worked and whom they could marry. This "protection" robbed the Aborigines of the rights and freedoms enjoyed by other British subjects. The other Australian colonies soon introduced similar laws.

1

2. It shall be lawful for the Governor from time to time to make regulations and orders . . .

(I.) For prescribing the place where any aboriginal or any tribe of aborigines shall reside.

(II.) For prescribing the terms on which contracts for and on behalf of aboriginals may be made with Europeans . . .

(III.) For apportioning amongst aboriginals the earnings of aboriginals under any contract . . .

(IV.) For the distribution and expenditure of moneys granted by Parliament for the benefit of aborigines.

(V.) For the care custody and education of the children of aborigines.

Aboriginal Protection Act, 1869

◀ Victoria's Aboriginal Protection Act set up the Board for the Protection of Aborigines and gave it the power to control every aspect of Aborigines' lives: where they could live, where they could work, how much they could be paid, and how their children should be educated. The board even took Aboriginal children from their homes, starting the process that separated thousands of children from their families.

2

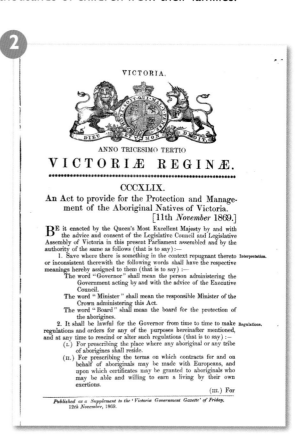

▶ The 1869 Aboriginal Protection Act took away the basic rights of Aboriginal people in Victoria and placed them under the control of white officials.

16

▶ *The Age,* a newspaper in Melbourne, Victoria, expresses its belief that the Aborigines were an inferior race who would die out. In the late 1800's, popular thinking applied a theory called *survival of the fittest* to society. According to the theory, natural processes favor the survival of the fittest members of society. The groups best able to survive acquire advanced technology. A lack of technology, according to the theory, proves a group's unfitness. Powerful groups used the theory to justify their domination over other groups, such as the Aborigines.

3

Human progress has all been achieved by the spread of the progressive races and the squeezing out of the inferior ones. No one can contend that it would have been better for the world had no European set foot on this continent and the blacks had been left to the chance of reaching civilisation by a slow course of natural development. It may be doubted whether the Australian aborigine would ever have advanced much beyond the status of the *neolithic races* [people who used stone, rather than metal, tools] in which we found him, and we need not therefore lament his disappearance.

The Age, 1888

4

◀ Four Aborigines who have been captured by the Queensland police in 1900 stand chained together under guard. The police dealt harshly with Aborigines who stole from or attacked settlers.

NOW YOU KNOW

- By the mid-1800's, starvation, disease, and conflict had greatly reduced the Aboriginal population.
- The colonies introduced laws to "protect," but really to control, the Aborigines.
- Many white people believed that "inferior" peoples, such as the Aborigines, would die out.

The Reserves

Beginning in the 1850's, the colonial governments removed many Aboriginal groups from their traditional lands and sent them to live in special government-funded settlements known as *reserves*. Life on the reserves offered little freedom. The Aborigines lived there under the control of white managers, who sometimes mistreated them. On the reserves, Aborigines had to abandon their traditional way of life and become farmers. They were forced to wear European clothes and were forbidden to practice their traditional ceremonies or speak their own languages. The worst reserves resembled prison camps.

1

So, yes, there was some come from the New South, some from Western District and some from up the Wimmera [a region in western Victoria], yes, they all come here and down Sale [a city in eastern Victoria] way, they were all drafted here. It was sort of like, what we used to say, we were like cattle. We were just drafted here and drafted wherever we were put, is where you had to stay, yes. . . .
Ivy Marks, 2003

◄ In a 2003 interview, Ivy Marks (1935?-) recalls how the Aborigines were forced to settle in places chosen for them by the authorities. Marks came to the Lake Tyers Aboriginal Reserve in Victoria when she was about 10 years old and has lived there all her life.

2

► An Aboriginal family on a reserve pose for a photograph in the late 1800's or early 1900's. The writing on the photo reads "rightful owners of the soil." However, most white settlers did not recognize the Aborigines' land rights. The Aborigines had no ownership of the reserves where they were forced to live.

18

3

We the undersigned have been living on Poonindie for a number of years. We are very sorry to hear that the place is to be taken from us. It is very hard to be turned away from what has been our home.

Aborigines of Poonindie Mission, 1894

◀ In an 1894 petition, Aborigines at Poonindie Mission, an Anglican mission on the Eyre Peninsula of South Australia, express their regret that the mission will be closed. They were forced to move from Poonindie because white settlers wanted their rich farmland.

▼ In the early 1900's, Aboriginal women and children stand outside their "settlement"—a collection of shacks—at Barambah Aboriginal Settlement (now Cherbourg) in Queensland. Many Aboriginal people lived in such miserable conditions.

4

NOW YOU KNOW

- Aborigines were forced to live in settlements called reserves in places white settlers did not want to occupy.
- On the reserves, Aborigines had little freedom and often lived in bad conditions.
- If white settlers decided they wanted reserve lands, the Aborigines had to move.

Christian Missions

CHRISTIANITY PLAYED AN IMPORTANT ROLE ON THE ABORIGINAL RESERVES. Many reserves were run directly by missionaries, whose goal was to convert people to Christianity. Most missionaries wanted to make life better for the Aborigines. But many also believed that the best way to help Aborigines was to make them abandon their traditional ways, convert them to Christianity, and force them to live like Europeans. Although many Aborigines did embrace Christianity and European customs, they often had to fight to obtain basic rations and facilities.

▶ The Aborigines of Point Macleay Mission Station (now Raukkan) on Lake Alexandrina in South Australia complain about their living conditions in a petition to the governor of the colony. They claim that government funds are spent on the white people at the mission. The Aborigines state that there is too much emphasis on religion and not enough on their everyday well-being. The Adelaide newspaper *The Advertiser* published their petition in 1907.

1

At present the true aborigines of the lakes [Lake Alexandrina and Lake Albert] get little or no benefit from the mission. All of the money your Government give us is spent on white officers and the half white population of the place. . . . Of course, the mission does a great deal of preaching and praying, but we old natives of the soil would do with less of that and more of food, clothes and better tents. In fact, we are too badly dressed to attend the church, and too ill-fed to think much about praying.

Aborigines of Point Macleay Mission Station, 1907

2

One of the first acts of reform I adopted . . . was to *induce* [persuade] them to marry according to our British laws. This they objected to at first, telling me they had been "married enough." By *judicious* [wise] and firm action, I then locked the store door, refusing them food unless they obeyed. After a few days of conference and empty stomachs, a *deputation* [delegation] waited upon me with the information they were willing to get married. Through taking this stand I was enabled to put a stop to their *illicit* [wrong] and unhappy relationships, and so brought in joy and contentment.

Daniel Matthews, 1899

◀ The English missionary Daniel Matthews (1837-1902) describes how he persuaded the Aborigines at Maloga Mission, New South Wales, to enter into Christian marriages. Matthews and other missionaries tried to stop traditional Aboriginal customs and ceremonies, which they saw as not only unchristian but also uncivilized. At Maloga Mission, which Matthews established in 1874, the Aborigines had to get up early, pray every day, and drink no alcohol.

20

▼ Aborigines attend a church service in the late 1800's at Ramahyuck Mission Station on Lake Wellington in Victoria. Despite the heavy-handed tactics of some missionaries, many Aborigines became devout Christians.

NOW YOU KNOW

- Christian missionaries ran many Aboriginal reserves.
- Some missionaries were more concerned with converting Aborigines to Christianity than with promoting their everyday well-being.
- Some missionaries used harsh methods to force Aborigines to live like Europeans.

Better and Worse: Coranderrk

I N 1863, THE ABORIGINES OF VICTORIA SET UP A RESERVE CALLED CORANDERRK ABORIGINAL STATION on the Yarra River. They built houses and a school for their children and planted crops. The station's first manager, the Scottish missionary John Green (1830?-1908), treated the residents fairly, and Coranderrk flourished. The Aborigines grew hops, wheat, and vegetables, and sold their produce in nearby Melbourne. But the Board for the Protection of Aborigines disapproved of the way Green ran the station and forced him to resign in 1874. After Green left, conditions at Coranderrk worsened. The Aborigines, led by William Barak (1818?-1903) of the Wurundjeri people, complained about their bad living conditions and lack of rights.

1

The station has never been improved since the old manager left. No clearing or grubbing done; no potatoes, cabbages, or other vegetables have been grown, and no fencing done. . . . Nothing has been put in the orchard, and vegetables have not been grown for the good of our health. Mr. Green was very neighborly, and . . . Mrs. Green was like a mother to all the natives. . . . Under Mr. Green we used to kill our own cattle, and grow our own potatoes, cabbages, onions, carrots and pumpkins—everything we could grow. We had plenty of milk, butter, and cheese. We get nothing like that now.

Thomas Bamfield, 1881

◀ A resident at Coranderrk Aboriginal Station, Thomas Bamfield (1844?-1893) of the Taungurong people, describes conditions there to a parliamentary board of inquiry in 1881. After John Green resigned, the Aborigines complained to the Board for the Protection of Aborigines about the lack of food and other bad conditions. In 1881, the government ordered an inquiry into the management of the station.

2

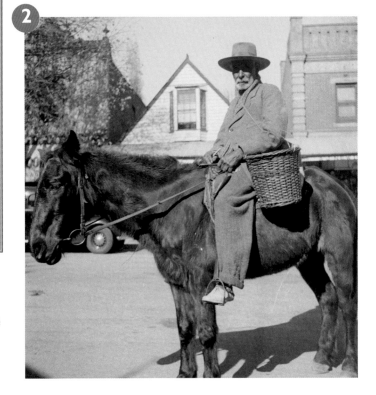

▶ William Barak of the Wurundjeri people was one of the founders of Coranderrk station and a leading campaigner for Aboriginal rights.

22

3

. . . could we get our freedom to go away . . . and to come home when we wish, and also to go for the good of our health when we need it; and we aboriginals all wish and hope to have freedom, not to be bound down by the protection of the board . . . we should be free like the White Population. There is only few Blacks now remaining in Victoria. We are all dying away now and we blacks of aboriginal blood wish to have now freedom for all our life time. . . .

Aborigines of Coranderrk, 1886

◀ William Barak and other Aboriginal residents of Coranderrk petition the government of Victoria for greater freedom in 1886. They wrote the petition in response to the Aboriginal Protection Act of 1886, called the Half-Caste Act. The law enabled the government to remove from Aboriginal reserves anyone under the age of 35 who was "half-caste" (of mixed Aboriginal and white ancestry). It broke up many Aboriginal families and communities. After it was passed, dozens of people were forced to leave Coranderrk because they had some white blood.

▼ An *idealized* (perfect rather than actual) drawing of a street in Coranderrk appeared in *The Illustrated London News,* a British magazine, on Jan. 12, 1889. Conditions were much worse than pictured.

4

STREET OF CORANDERRK, THE ABORIGINES' STATION, VICTORIA.

NOW YOU KNOW

- In 1863, the Aborigines set up Coranderrk Aboriginal Station, and at first it flourished.
- In the mid-1870's, the Board for the Protection of Aborigines changed how Coranderrk was run, and conditions there grew worse.
- The people of Coranderrk complained about the mismanagement of the station and their lack of rights, but the authorities ignored them.

Aborigines as Nonpersons

IN 1901, THE SIX AUSTRALIAN COLONIES JOINED TOGETHER TO FORM the Commonwealth of Australia. The colonies became states within the Commonwealth. A ceremony in Sydney celebrated the birth of the Australian nation. But the Aborigines—the first Australians—had no significant role in the celebration. The new nation was progressive in many ways. In 1902, it gave white women the right to vote in federal elections. In the early 1900's, laws laid down a minimum wage for work and created a government pension for old people. But Aborigines remained nonpersons, receiving none of these rights or benefits.

▲ On Jan. 1, 1901, Sydney celebrated the birth of the federation of Australia. A huge parade through the city ended in a great ceremony in Centennial Park to mark the *inauguration* (formal beginning) of the Commonwealth. Hundreds of thousands of Australians watched the ceremony, but no Aborigines were invited to take part.

24

2

51 (xxvi). The Parliament shall, subject to this Constitution, have power to make laws for the peace, order, and good government of the Commonwealth with respect to . . . people of any race, other than the aboriginal race in any State, for whom it is deemed necessary to make special laws . . .

127. In reckoning the numbers of the people of the Commonwealth, or of a State or other part of the Commonwealth, aboriginal natives shall not be counted.

*Commonwealth of Australia
Constitution Act 1900*

◀ The Constitution of Australia, the document that describes how the new system of government would operate, sets up a federal Parliament to make laws for the nation. But Section 51 (xxvi) of the Constitution declares that the laws passed by Parliament will not apply to Aboriginal people. Section 127 declares that Aborigines will not be counted when the government takes a census. Constitutional amendments in 1967 removed the words "other than the aboriginal race in any State" from section 51 and withdrew all of section 127.

▶ An article in *The Sydney Morning Herald* in 1905 points out that Australia's new Constitution prohibits the federal government from making laws and policies for Aborigines. Instead, it leaves the care of the Aborigines to the state governments. As a result, the laws under which the Aborigines lived, and the way they were treated, varied greatly from state to state. Many Aborigines suffered from poverty and alcoholism.

3

Drunkenness, disease, and immorality are prevalent among these unfortunate people. . . . the *indigent* [needy] aborigines are victimised by dishonest ration-distributors, *half-caste* [mixed race] children are left to a life of *vagabondage* [wandering]. . . . This is a sad state of affairs, and a reflection on our civilisation. . . . The care of the aborigines is a State and not a Federal concern, since the 26th definition of the powers of Parliament restricts these to "the people of any race other than the aboriginal race in any State."

*The Sydney Morning
Herald, 1905*

NOW YOU KNOW

- In 1901, the Australian colonies formed the Commonwealth of Australia.
- Aboriginal people did not receive the same rights as other Australians.
- The new Commonwealth of Australia viewed the Aborigines as nonpersons. They were not even counted in the census.

The Stolen Generations

BEGINNING IN THE LATE 1800'S, officials in the Australian states took Aboriginal children from their families and placed them under the care of whites in institutions and foster homes. In particular, the officials separated mixed-race children from "blacks," hoping that the children would be absorbed by the white population. Aboriginal culture, they believed, would then die out. Police and welfare officers took away up to 100,000 Aboriginal children, especially those who had some European ancestry or had pale skin. The children's families never knew where they had gone. These children later became known as the "stolen generations."

▶ The Aborigines Protection Act passed by New South Wales in 1909 gives the state government the right to seize any Aboriginal child or any "neglected" mixed-race child. In reality, the authorities removed many Aboriginal children from loving families. The children were raised in institutions called *half-caste homes,* where they suffered from neglect, hunger, disease, and abuse.

1

It shall be the duty of the [Aborigines Protection] board . . . to provide for the custody, maintenance, and education of the children of aborigines. . . . The board may . . . cause to be *bound* [put under contract as an apprentice learning a trade from a skilled master] the child of any aborigine, or the neglected child of any person apparently having an *admixture* [mixture] of aboriginal blood in his veins to be apprenticed to any master. . . . Every child so apprenticed shall be under the supervision of the board . . .

Aborigines Protection Act, 1909

2

Homes Are Sought For These Children

A GROUP OF TINY HALF-CASTE AND QUADROON CHILDREN at the Darwin half-caste home. The Minister for the Interior (Mr Perkins) recently appealed to charitable organisations in Melbourne and Sydney to find homes for the children and rescue them from becoming outcasts.

I like the little girl in Centre of group, but if taken by anyone else, any of the others would do, as long as they are strong

◀ A photograph of mixed-race children available to foster homes in the 1930's was printed by a newspaper in Darwin, Northern Territory. Officials took "half-caste and *quadroon*" (one-fourth Aboriginal) children from their families and sent them to institutions or foster homes as if they were orphans. The writing below the photo reads, "I like the little girl in centre of group, but if taken by anyone else, any of the others would do, as long as they are strong." This comment suggests that a child was being taken to be put to work as a servant or farm hand.

3

Are we going to have a population of 1,000,000 blacks in the Commonwealth [of Australia], or are we going to merge them into our white community and eventually forget that there ever were any aborigines in Australia?

A. O. Neville, 1937

◄ Auber Octavius (A. O.) Neville (1875-1954), an English-born government official, asks a national conference of Aboriginal administrators in Canberra in 1937 what their goal should be. Neville served first as chief protector of Aborigines and then as commissioner for native affairs for the state of Western Australia. At the 1937 conference, he and his colleagues adopted a nationwide policy of making the Aborigines part of white society so that they would eventually disappear. The conference called for taking mixed-race children from Aboriginal families so that the children would live as white people.

▶ A photograph shows how the policy of absorbing mixed-race people was supposed to work. The grandmother, *far right,* had an Aboriginal mother and a white father. With her are her daughter and her grandson. Each generation has become "whiter" than the last by marrying into the white community. The intended final result of the policy was that the descendants of Aborigines would look and behave like white people.

4

THREE GENERATIONS
(Reading from Right to Left)

1. Half-blood—(Irish-Australian father; full-blood Aboriginal mother).
2. Quadroon Daughter—(Father Australian born of Scottish parents; Mother No. 1).
3. Octaroon Grandson—(Father Australian of Irish descent; Mother No. 2).

NOW YOU KNOW

- Starting in the late 1800's, the Australian states attempted to absorb mixed-race children into white society.
- Officials removed up to 100,000 children from Aboriginal families as if they were orphans.
- These children are known as the "stolen generations."

Organizing for Rights

STARTING IN THE 1920'S, ABORIGINES BEGAN TO ORGANIZE POLITICAL GROUPS to demand the same rights as other Australians. Aboriginal rights organizations protested the unjust treatment of Aboriginal people, including their loss of lands to white farmers, poor living conditions on the reserves, and the forced removal of Aboriginal children. The groups wrote to newspapers, organized petition drives, and held public meetings and rallies.

1

The A.A.P.A. has been formed – the letters stand for the Australian Aboriginal Progressive Association, and they have at present two objectives . . .

First – That the aboriginal will be given a small portion of land in his own right to build his home upon. A five or ten acre [2 or 4 hectare] lot is asked for in a suitable locality.

Second – They beg that their homes will no longer be despoiled [robbed]; but that they may be allowed to keep their children with them and develop them. . . .

Elizabeth McKenzie Hatton, 1925

◀ Elizabeth McKenzie Hatton (1870?-1944), a white Australian missionary and social worker, tells readers of *The Voice of the North* newspaper in northern New South Wales about the aims of the Australian Aboriginal Progressive Association (AAPA)—land of their own and the right to keep their own children. Hatton served as secretary of the AAPA, one of the first Aboriginal rights groups in Australia.

2

PETITION.

of the Aboriginal Inhabitants of Australia to His Majesty King George V . . . YOUR PETITIONERS therefore humbly pray that Your Majesty will intervene on our behalf . . . To prevent the extinction of the Aboriginal Race . . . and grant us power to propose a member of parliament in the person of our own Blood, or White man known to have studied our needs and to be in Sympathy with our Race to represent us in the Federal Parliament.

William Cooper, 1934

▶ A petition to the British king asks that a seat in the Australian Parliament be set aside for an Aborigine or a white man sympathetic to them. The Aboriginal leader William Cooper (1860?-1941) organized the petition. From 1934 to 1938, he collected the signatures of more than 1,800 Aborigines on the document. In 1936, Cooper helped found the Australian Aborigines' League (AAL) in Victoria.

▶ *The Australian Abo Call,* the first Aboriginal-run newspaper in Australia, debuted in April 1938. The Aboriginal journalist John T. (Jack) Patten, Jr., (1904-1957) edited the paper. It appeared monthly for only six issues before lack of funding forced Patten to cease publication. Today, *Abo* is an offensive term for an Aboriginal person.

The Australian ABO CALL
THE VOICE OF THE ABORIGINES
EDITED BY J. T. PATTEN

Representing 80,000 Australian Aborigines

We ask for Education, Opportunity, and Full Citizen Rights

No. 1 — MONTHLY, 3d. — APRIL, 1938.

To all Aborigines!

"The Abo Call" is our own paper.

It has been established to present the case for aborigines, from the point of view of the Aborigines themselves.

This paper has nothing to do with missionaries, or anthropologists, or with anybody who looks down on Aborigines as an "Inferior" race.

We are NOT an inferior race, we have merely been refused the chance of education that whites receive. "The Abo Call" will show that we do not want to go back to the stone Age.

Representing 60,000 Full Bloods and 20,000 Halfcastes in Australia, we raise our voice to ask for education, Equal Opportunity, and Full Citizen Rights.

"The Abo Call" will be published once a month. Price 3d.

The Editor asks all Aborigines and Halfcastes to support the paper, by buying it and also by acting as agents for sale to white friends and supporters.

Please send postal note when ordering copies.

Address all letters to: –
J.T. Patten, "The Abo Call", Box 1924 KK, General Post Office, Sydney, N.S.W.

OUR TEN POINTS

Deputation to the Prime Minister

The following is a full copy of the statement made to the prime Minister at the Deputation of the Aborigines on 31st January last.

The Prime Minister was accompanied by Dame Enid Lyons and by Mr. McEwan, Minister of the interior.

The Deputation consisted of twenty Aborigines, men and women, and Mr. Lyons gave a hearing of two hours to the statement of our case.

Please read these "ten points" carefully, as this is the only official statement of our aims and objects that has yet been made.

TO THE RIGHT HON. THE PRIME MINISTER OF AUSTRALIA.
MR. J.A. LYONS, P.C., C.H., M.H.R.
Sir,

In respectfully placing before you the following POLICY FOR ABORIGINES. We wish to state that this policy has been endorsed by a Conference of Aborigines, held in Sydney on 26th January of this year. This policy is the only policy which has the support of the Aborigines themselves.

URGENT INTERIM POLICY

A LONG RANGE POLICY FOR ABORIGINES.

1. – We respectfully request that there should be a National Policy for Aborigines. We advocate Commonwealth Government control of all Aboriginal affairs.

2. – We suggest the appointment of a Commonwealth Ministry for Aboriginal Affairs, the Minister to have full Cabinet rank.

3. – We suggest the appointment of an Administrative Head of the proposed Department of Aboriginal Affairs, the Administrator to be advised by an Advisory Board, consisting of six persons, three of whom at least should be of Aboriginal blood, to be nominated by the Aborigines Progressive Association.

4. – The aim of the Department of Aboriginal Affairs should be to *raise all Aborigines throughout the Commonwealth to full Citizen Status* and civil equality with the whites in Australia. In particular, and without delay, all Aborigines should be entitled:

(a) To receive the same educational opportunities as white people.

(b) To receive the benefits of labour legislation, including Arbitration Court Awards, on an equality with white workers.

Photo by courtesy "Man" Magazine

AT THE CONFERENCE OF 26th JANUARY.

T. Foster (La Perouse), J. Kinchela (Coonabarabran), W. Cooper (Melbourne), · D. Nicholls (Melbourne), J. T. Patten (La Perouse), W. Ferguson (Dubbo).

6. – We recommend that Aborigines should be entitled to the same privileges regarding housing as are white workers.

7. – We recommend that a special policy of Land Settlement for Aborigines should be put into operation, whereby Aborigines who desire to settle on the land should be given the same encouragement as that given to Immigrants or Soldier Settlers, with expert tuition in agriculture, and financial assistance to enable such settlers to become ultimately self-supporting.

8. – In regard to uncivilised and semi-civilised Aborigines, we suggest that patrol officers, nurses and teachers, both men and women, of *Aboriginal blood,* should be specially trained by the Commonwealth Government as Aboriginal Officers, to bring the wild people into contact with civilisation.

9. – We recommend that all Aboriginal and Halfcaste women should be entitled to maternity and free hospital treatment during confinement, and that there should be no discrimination against Aboriginal women, who should be entitled to clinical instruction on baby welfare, similar to that given to white women.

10. – While opposing a policy of segregation, we urge that, during a period of transition, the present Aboriginal Reserves should be retained as a sanctuary for aged or incompetent Aborigines who may be unfitted to take their place in the white community, owing to the past policy of neglect.

EASTER MEETING

A general meeting of Aborigines will be held at La Perouse Reserve on Easter Sunday (17th April).

The main purpose of the meeting is to adopt a Constitution and Rules for the Aborigines Progressive Association, also election of officers.

Please make a big effort to attend this important meeting, which will put our fight for Citizen Rights on a proper legal footing.

SELECT COMMITTEE

The Select Committee upon the Administration of the Aborigines Protection Board (New South Wales) took a lot of evidence, and then dissolved without making a report.

The Select Committee was a farce, as most of the evidence concerned the dismissal of Manager Brain from Brewarrina, and there was no time to present full evidence about the conditions of the 10.000 Aborigines and Halfcastes of New South Wales.

Parliament was more worried about one white man than about ten thousand blacks.

We call for a Royal Commission to investigate Aboriginal Administration in N.S.W.

We have a big lot of evidence, some of which will be published in "The Abo Call" in future numbers.

MR. BRUXNER'S PROMISE

In his policy speech in the N.S.W.

NOW YOU KNOW

- Beginning in the 1920's, Aboriginal people formed political groups to campaign for their rights.

- The aims of the groups included securing enough land for Aborigines to live on and gaining the right to raise their own children.

- Aboriginal groups campaigned for their rights by writing to newspapers and organizing petitions.

Day of Mourning

In 1938, Australia celebrated 150 years of British settlement. The anniversary was January 26, a national holiday known as Australia Day. Aboriginal groups in southeastern Australia, led by William Cooper, Jack Patten, and William Ferguson (1892-1950), declared that Australia Day would be a Day of Mourning. They used the occasion to tell the world what colonization of their land had meant for Aboriginal people. They distributed leaflets and explained their point of view in the press. When the day itself arrived, they held the first national Aboriginal civil rights gathering in Australian Hall in Sydney.

▶ Jack Patten explains to a gathering of Aboriginal people in Sydney on Jan. 26, 1938, why his people have no reason to celebrate the national holiday of Australia Day. Patten and the other organizers of the Day of Mourning viewed Australia Day, the anniversary of British settlement, as the anniversary of a disaster.

1

On this day the white people are rejoicing, but we, as Aborigines, have no reason to rejoice on Australia's 150th birthday. . . . This land belonged to our forefathers 150 years ago, but today we are pushed further and further into the background. . . . Aborigines throughout Australia are literally being starved to death.

Jack Patten, 1938

2

◀ Aboriginal people gather outside Australian Hall in Sydney on the Day of Mourning, Jan. 26, 1938. The conference was attended by hundreds of Aboriginal people.

30

3

AUSTRALIAN ABORIGINES CONFERENCE
Sesqui-Centenary

DAY OF MOURNING & PROTEST

to be held in

THE AUSTRALIAN HALL, SYDNEY
(No. 148 Elizabeth Street)

on

WEDNESDAY, 26th JANUARY, 1938

(Australia Day)

from

10 a.m. to 5 p.m.

THE FOLLOWING RESOLUTION WILL BE MOVED:

"WE, representing THE ABORIGINES OF AUSTRALIA, assembled in Conference at the Australian Hall, Sydney, on the 26th day of January, 1938, this being the 150th Anniversary of the whitemen's seizure of our country, HEREBY MAKE PROTEST against the callous treatment of our people by the whitemen during the past 150 years, AND WE APPEAL to the Australian Nation of today to make new laws for the education and care of Aborigines, and we ask for a new policy which will raise our people to FULL CITIZEN STATUS and EQUALITY WITHIN THE COMMUNITY."

Aborigines and Persons of Aboriginal Blood only are invited to attend. Please come if you can!

Signed for and on behalf of
THE ABORIGINES PROGRESSIVE ASSOCIATION

J. T. Patten, President.
W. Ferguson, Organising Secretary

Address: c/o Box 1924 KK
General Post Office, Sydney

▲ A leaflet advertises the Day of Mourning conference to be held in Sydney on Jan. 26th, 1938, the 150th anniversary of the "white man's seizure of our country." The conference was the first national Aboriginal civil rights meeting.

4

Without delay, all Aborigines should be entitled:

(a) To receive the same educational opportunities as white people.

(b) To receive the benefits of labour legislation . . . on an equality with white workers.

(c) To receive the full benefits of *workers' compensation* [payments for workers injured on the job] and insurance.

(d) To receive the benefits of old-age and invalid pensions, whether living in Aboriginal settlements or not.

(e) To own land and property, and to be allowed to save money in personal banking accounts . . .

(f) To receive wages in cash, and not by *orders* [vouchers], issue of rations, or apprenticeship systems.

Statement presented to Prime Minister
Joseph Lyons by Aborigine leaders, 1938

▲ A statement presented to Australian Prime Minister Joseph Lyons lists demands developed at the Day of Mourning conference. A group of about 20 Aboriginal leaders, including William Ferguson and Jack Patten, gave the list to the prime minister on Jan. 31, 1938. Lyons seemed to listen carefully, but nothing was done to meet the Aborigines' demands.

NOW YOU KNOW

- Aboriginal leaders used the 1938 celebration of white Australia's 150th anniversary to stage a protest they called the Day of Mourning.

- The protest helped draw attention to the wrongs done to Aborigines.

- A group of Aboriginal representatives met with the prime minister to propose reforms, but he did not act on their proposals.

Cummeragunja Walk-Off

THE GOVERNMENT OF NEW SOUTH WALES ESTABLISHED CUMMERAGUNJA MISSION in 1881 on the banks of the Murray River. The mission lay just inside New South Wales, close to the border with Victoria. At first, the community prospered. But in 1915, the Aborigines Protection Board of New South Wales began removing mixed-race children. As had happened at Coranderrk in the 1870's, conditions at the reserve worsened. By Feb. 4, 1939, the Aborigines, mostly Yorta Yorta people, had had enough. More than 150 of them staged a walk-off. They left the reserve and crossed into Victoria, where they set up camps.

1

The conditions at Cummeroogunga [Cummeragunja] are shocking. The rations issued by the administration are often rotten — not fit for pigs to eat. Housing and sanitary conditions are vile. . . . The people at Cummeroogunga lived in constant fear of their children being taken away from them by the Board, and being placed in homes. Wholesale kidnapping (it was nothing less) occurred on the Mission only a few years ago. The Manager sent the aboriginal men away on a rabbiting expedition. . . . No sooner had they left the station than car loads of police (who had been waiting) dashed in and seized all the children they could get their hands on.

Margaret Tucker, 1939

◀ The Aboriginal leader Margaret Tucker (1904-1996) describes the terrible living conditions at Cummeragunja Mission in a 1939 letter to *Worker's Voice*, a Communist Party newspaper published in Victoria. The Aboriginal people living there suffered from poverty and disease and the fear that their children would be taken away from them.

2

John Thomas Patten, *compositor* [typesetter], of Redfern, Sydney, was charged with having *enticed* [lured] and persuaded aborigines to leave the Cummeragunja Mission Station at Barmah, N.S.W. . . . Patten said . . . he had never tried to *induce* [persuade] residents of Cummeragunja to leave the reserve. He believed that the people left because of . . . the manager "who drove round with a rifle on his *lorry* [truck] and looked at them in a hostile manner." Mr. Hawkins [the judge] said that he was satisfied with the police evidence. . . . He believed that Patten frightened and incited people with the inevitable consequences that they left.

The Argus, 1939

▶ A report in the Melbourne newspaper *The Argus* describes the trial and conviction of the Aboriginal leader Jack Patten in March 1939. Patten had gone to Cummeragunja earlier that year to talk to the residents. The mission manager viewed him as a trouble-maker and called in the police. The police arrested Patten and charged him with "incitement"—that is, persuading the Aborigines to leave the reserve—though they had every reason to go. Judges usually accepted the versions of events given by the police and station managers, so Patten was found guilty.

32

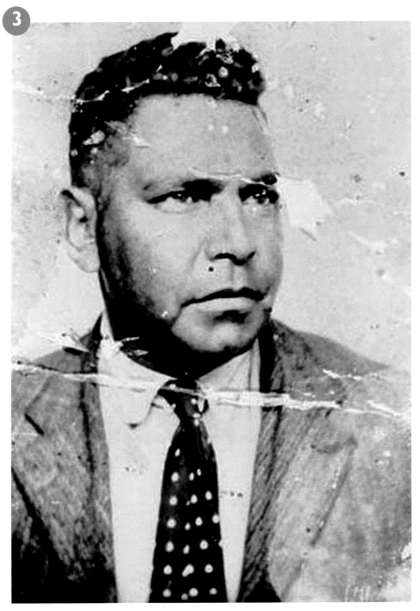

◀ The Aboriginal leader and journalist Jack Patten was born on the Cummeragunja Mission. He edited *The Australian Abo Call,* the first Aboriginal-run newspaper. He also played a leading role in organizing the Day of Mourning protests and conference in 1938. In addition, Patten cofounded the Aborigines Progressive Association (APA) in 1938 and served as its first president.

NOW YOU KNOW

- As at many Aboriginal reserves, conditions at Cummeragunja Mission were terrible.
- The residents of the Cummeragunja Mission staged a walk-off in February 1939.
- The authorities blamed the Aboriginal leader Jack Patten for the walk-off.

Work and Wages

AS WHITE SETTLEMENT EXPANDED, MANY ABORIGINES ABANDONED their traditional way of life. They settled on reserves or took jobs with white employers. They provided cheap labor on farms and ranches and as domestic servants. Often they received no wages. Even by the late 1940's, half of all Aboriginal *stockmen* (ranch workers) were not paid. White landowners paid only for such necessities as food and clothing and for a license to employ the Aborigines. The license cost 5 shillings (about U.S. $1) and was less expensive than a dog license. In the 1940's, some Aboriginal workers began to fight for their rights.

▶ The Aboriginal leader Pearl Gibbs (1901-1983) reminds Australians in a radio broadcast of the role that her people played in building their nation. In this broadcast, made in 1941, during World War II (1939-1945), she points out that Aborigines have served their country and so should be treated as full citizens. Gibbs was a leader of the Aborigines Progressive Association (APA).

You will also agree with me that Australia . . . could not have been opened up successfully without my people's help and guidance of the white explorers. Hundreds of white men, women and children owe their very lives to Aborigine trackers and runners—tracking lost people. Quite a few airmen owe their lives to Aboriginals. I want you to remember that men of my race served . . . in the 1914-18 War [World War I] and today hundreds of full-bloods . . . and half-castes are overseas. . . . My own son is somewhere on the high seas serving with the Australian Navy. . . . So we are asking for full citizenship.

Pearl Gibbs, 1941

◀ Clancy McKenna (1909-1979) and Dooley Bin Bin (1896-1982), two Aborigines of the Nyamil people, led the first major strike of Aboriginal stock workers. On May 1, 1946, some 600 to 800 Aboriginal stockmen in the Pilbara region of Western Australia walked off the job. They demanded better pay and the right to form unions. The strike ended in a victory for the workers in 1949.

▲ Aboriginal stockmen, or ranch workers, received either little pay or no cash wages at all. Their cheap labor helped white farmers make big profits from raising sheep and cattle.

NOW YOU KNOW

- Aboriginal labor helped the settlers colonize Australia and build its sheep and cattle industries.
- Aborigines served in Australia's armed forces in World War I (1914-1918) and World War II (1939-1945).
- In 1946, workers in the Pilbara region staged the first successful Aboriginal strike.

Assimilation and Discrimination

By the 1940's and 1950's, the policies of state Aborigine protection boards had shifted. They increasingly emphasized persuading Aborigines to adopt the values and habits of the white majority. This process is called *assimilation.* To gain the rights of other citizens, Aborigines had to give up their own culture and behave as white people did. Many Aborigines did not want to give up their identity. Meanwhile, they suffered *discrimination* (poor treatment because of their race). They had fewer opportunities in education and work and were paid less for doing the same jobs as whites. The Aborigines also were *segregated* (kept separate) in many public places, such as swimming pools and movie theaters.

1

...I got a job at Greenmount boarding house, that is when I noticed the racism. I could only work in the kitchens, me and my Aboriginal friends. I would've liked to have been a waitress but we weren't allowed out in the dining room. ...Then when you go into the shops, you could be standing next in line to be served, they'd look all over you, they'd serve all around you, they wouldn't serve you. . . . They'd just serve all the other white people in front of you. . . .

Beulah Pickwick, 2009

◀ An elderly Aboriginal woman remembers what life was like in her youth in Queensland and New South Wales. As her recollections show, racism was not just practiced by governments and officials. Ordinary people, such as boarding house owners and shop clerks, also held racist attitudes.

2

THIS IS TO CERTIFY that _____ Aborigine, aged _____ years, residing at ____ is a person who in the opinion of the Aborigines Welfare Board [formerly the New South Wales Aborigines Protection Board], ought no longer be subject to the provisions/following provisions of the Aborigines Protection Act and Regulations, or any such provisions, and he/she is accordingly exempted from such provisions.

certificate of exemption from the Aborigines Protection Act, 1943

▶ Beginning in the 1940's, state governments gave citizenship rights to some Aborigines under certain conditions. They had to give up their traditional ways, live as Europeans, and keep away from other Aborigines who still lived on reserves. The Aborigines who agreed to these conditions received papers called *exemption certificates* or *citizenship certificates.* The certificates allowed them to vote, move around freely, find employment, and stay out as late as they wanted. The Aborigines called the certificates "dog tags," which shows how angry they felt about needing special permission to enjoy basic freedoms.

▲ In 1940, soldiers in an all-Aboriginal volunteer platoon stand at attention in their camp at Wangaratta, Victoria. At the beginning of World War II (1939-1945), the Australian Military Forces refused to enlist people "not substantially of European origin or descent." But the threat of a Japanese invasion changed official policy, and thousands of Aborigines and Torres Island people joined the armed services.

NOW YOU KNOW

- In the 1940's and 1950's, Aboriginal people remained at a disadvantage when compared with other Australians.
- The Australian government tried to encourage Aborigines to give up their culture and adopt the white way of life.
- Certificates of exemption freed some Aborigines from the restrictions placed on them, but only on condition that they blended into white society.

Organizing Nationally

IN 1958, ABORIGINAL RIGHTS LEADERS FOUNDED A NEW NATIONAL ORGANIZATION, the Federal Council for Aboriginal Advancement (FCAA). The FCAA, the first Aboriginal organization to operate across the entire country, campaigned for the rights of all the Aboriginal people of Australia. In 1964, the FCAA became the Federal Council for the Advancement of Aborigines and Torres Strait Islanders (FCAATSI). The Torres Strait Islands lie just north of Queensland and are part of Australia. The islanders are an ethnically different group from Aborigines. Often, when people talk about Aborigines and Torres Strait Islanders together, they describe both peoples as *indigenous* (original) Australians.

▶ At the founding conference of the FCAA in 1958, the Aboriginal leader Herbert (Bert) Groves (1907-1970) explains why he opposes the policy of assimilation. Groves and other Aboriginal leaders believed their people could be productive, equal citizens while still maintaining their identity and traditions.

1

But what does it [assimilation] imply? Certainly, citizenship and equal status . . . but also the disappearance of the Aborigines as a separate cultural group, and ultimately their physical absorption by the European part of the population. It is assumed that if Aborigines are going to lead the same kind of life as other Australians, then they must disappear as a distinct group. We feel that the word "integration" [joining together] implies a truer definition of our aims and objects.

Bert Groves, 1958

2

◀ During a demonstration in 1965, the Aboriginal poet Kath Walker (1920-1993) reads from her book *We Are Going* (1964). Walker, who later took the Aboriginal name Oodgeroo Noonucal, was the first Aboriginal woman to have a book published. She became a leading member of FCAATSI.

3

We realise of course that some Aborigines are prepared to accept assimilation, but what we object to is "forced assimilation."... The people of Lake Tyers have been ... advocating [arguing] for a new deal. ... This has prompted the government here to step up their assimilation policy, with promises of housing and employment in Towns surrounding Lake Tyers. Some people have accepted this offer, but again we don't want this forced on the people who do not wish to leave Lake Tyers ... the FCAA has been most concerned over the filching [stealing] of Reserves in other States and we would not like the same thing to happen to Lake Tyers and the people dispossessed.

Joe McGinness, May 22, 1963

◀ Joe McGinness (1914-2003), an Aboriginal wharf worker and civil rights leader, explains at a 1963 meeting why he thinks the Lake Tyers Mission should remain open. In 1962, the government of Victoria had announced plans to close Lake Tyers, an Aboriginal reserve in the eastern part of the state. Protests against the closing of Aboriginal reserves soon expanded into a national movement for Aboriginal land rights.

▼ Doug Nicholls (1906-1988) leads a protest in 1965 against plans to remove the Aboriginal people from the Lake Tyers Mission in Victoria. In 1972, Nicholls was the first Aborigine to be knighted, becoming Sir Douglas Nicholls. He served as governor of South Australia in 1976 and 1977.

4

NOW YOU KNOW

- The Federal Council for Aboriginal Advancement (FCAA) brought together Aboriginal people from across Australia to campaign for rights.
- Australia has two *indigenous* (original) peoples, the Aborigines and the Torres Strait Islanders.
- The FCAA campaigned against the closing of the Lake Tyers Mission, an Aboriginal reserve.

Protesting Racism

CHARLES PERKINS (1936-2000) WAS THE FIRST ABORIGINAL STUDENT AT THE UNIVERSITY OF SYDNEY. In 1965, he led a rights campaign called the Freedom Ride. It was inspired by the African American civil rights movement in the United States. Perkins and a group of white students traveled around Australia in a bus, drawing attention to racism and segregation. They protested outside social clubs, swimming pools, and other places where whites and Aboriginals were kept separate. The Freedom Ride won publicity for the cause of Aboriginal rights and drew attention to racism in Australia. Students from other universities went on to mount similar protests.

1

150 years of persecution, extermination, indifference, prejudice, discrimination... "welfare" policies and sheer neglect have left the original Australians as a depressed racial minority. This ... situation is ignored by ... society. The community's conscience MUST be awakened by protest action. This has succeeded in the USA—it could do so here.

Sydney University Organising Committee for Action on Aboriginal Rights, 1964

◀ A leaflet from the Sydney University Organising Committee for Action on Aboriginal Rights advertises a 1964 meeting to protest the racist policies of the Australian government. Many members of this group went on to take part in the Freedom Ride.

2

▶ University of Sydney students belonging to a group called Student Action for Aborigines—also known as the Freedom Riders—pose beside the bus that they hired for their February 1965 protest tour of New South Wales.

40

▶ A Sydney newspaper describes the violence that erupted in the New South Wales town of Moree in February 1965 after Freedom Riders tried to take Aboriginal children into a public swimming pool. The students visited Moree to draw attention to segregation at the local swimming pools, which Aborigines could not use at the same time as white people.

3

White women jeered and spat at girl freedom riders today as racial violence broke out for the first time at Moree. The students were pushed and carried from the front door of the Moree *baths* [swimming pool] while an angry crowd of 500 booed and catcalled . . . . The trouble erupted when 27 young men and women from Sydney University tried to escort six Aboriginal children into the baths.

Sunday Mirror, 1965

4

◀ The Australian cartoonist John Frith (1906-2000) shows an Aboriginal father painting his children white to enable them to visit a segregated swimming pool. Frith's cartoon appeared in *The Herald,* a newspaper in Melbourne, Victoria, on Feb. 20, 1965.

NOW YOU KNOW

- During the early 1960's, students became involved in protesting Australian racism.
- In 1965, the Freedom Riders traveled around New South Wales protesting in towns where Aboriginal people were segregated from whites.
- At Moree, New South Wales, people assaulted student protesters who tried to take Aboriginal children into the swimming pool.

Australians Say "Yes"

During the 1960's, Aboriginal rights groups led a campaign demanding citizenship rights for Aborigines. The campaigners organized petitions and distributed pamphlets. Their pressure persuaded the government to hold a *referendum* (vote of all the people on a single issue). The referendum asked voters whether they wanted to abolish the parts of the Constitution that barred Aboriginal people from full citizenship rights. In the vote, on May 27, 1967, a remarkable 90.77 percent of the voters said "yes." The Aboriginal population would now be counted in the census, and the federal Parliament's laws would apply to them.

▶ Shirley Andrews (1915-2001), an Australian biochemist and campaigner for Aboriginal rights, reports that the Federal Council for Aboriginal Advancement (FCAA) will launch a national petition drive to *amend* (change) Australia's Constitution. The drive by the FCAA—later called the Federal Council for the Advancement of Aborigines and Torres Strait Islanders (FCAATSI)—persuaded Parliament to approve an amendment revising Section 51 and removing Section 127 of the Constitution. Those sections had prevented the federal government from making laws applying to Aboriginal people and had barred them from being counted in a census. Voters approved the bill in a 1967 referendum.

1

The last Annual Meeting of the Federal Council for Aboriginal Advancement decided on an Australia wide petition calling for a referendum to amend the Federal Constitution so as to delete the clauses which discriminate against Aborigines.

Shirley Andrews, 1962

2

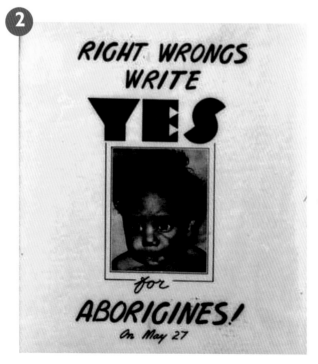

◀ A poster encourages Australians to vote "yes" in the referendum on Aboriginal rights on May 27, 1967.

42

3

Mr Onus said Australians must vote to give the Aborigine full citizenship rights. It was a basic question of human rights. "The referendum must be passed," he said. "The image of Australia throughout the world is at stake. If it is not passed, Australia will be held up to ridicule."

The Age, 1967

◀ William T. (Bill) Onus, Jr., (1906-1968) of the Aborigines Advancement League (AAL) emphasizes in a newspaper interview the difference the referendum would make to Australia's place in the world. By the 1960's, people worldwide cared about human rights. If a country mistreated its own people or minority groups, it risked becoming isolated.

4

◀ In Sydney Town Hall, an Aboriginal woman casts her vote in the 1967 referendum. As a result of the referendum, Aborigines were counted in the national census in 1971, for the first time. Once they were counted, they had the right to vote in elections for the federal Parliament.

NOW YOU KNOW

- During the 1960's, rights groups campaigned for Aborigines to gain full citizenship rights.
- In a 1967 referendum, an overwhelming majority of Australians voted to give Aboriginal people full citizenship.
- For the first time, Aborigines gained the right to vote in federal elections.

Strike and Walkout

In 1966, Aboriginal workers belonging to the Gurindji people went on strike at Newcastle Waters and Wave Hill cattle *stations* (ranches) in the Northern Territory. The strike began as a protest against bad conditions and low pay, but it grew into a demand for the return of traditional Gurindji lands. The workers, led by Vincent Lingiari (1908-1988), staged a walk-off and set up a new community at Wattie Creek, which they called Daguragu. The strikers held out for nearly nine years. In 1975, the Australian government met some of their demands. Their action marked the beginning of a movement for land rights.

1

"We not going back for you. You never treat us proper way. We can't go back to you because you rob we *bela* ["black fella," meaning Aborigines]. You never paid we bela proper wages, you never do good thing for we mob." Like that we say. That's that. Last time, we told him. "No, we not going back. We not working any more you station."

Ida Bernard, 1996

◀ Interviewed in 1996 for a magazine, Ida Bernard, a Gurindji kitchen worker, describes the anger of the Aboriginal workers at the way they had been treated at Wave Hill Station. Bernard worked at Wave Hill in the Northern Territory until the 1966 strike.

▼ Aborigines protest a proposed Northern Territory law in February 1968 that would have required them to pay rent for reserve lands. The protesters did not believe Aborigines should have to pay rent to use their own lands. More importantly, they did not want the lands to be sold, but to belong to their people forever.

2

3

The immediate *catalyst* [cause] of the strike was the refusal of the Vesteys' manager at Wave Hill to meet Vincent Lingiari's request that Aboriginal stockmen be paid $25 a week. But what was apparently an industrial dispute over appalling working and living conditions soon revealed itself to be something strikingly different: it was a demand from the Gurindji people for the return of their traditional lands. . . . When Lord Vestey attempted to get the Gurindji people to leave Wattie Creek and return to work on the station with inducements including money and wages, Vincent Lingiari told him: "You can keep your gold. We just want our land back."

Warren Snowdon, 2002

▶ On Aug. 16, 1975, Prime Minister Gough Whitlam (1916-) pours soil into the hands of strike organizer Vincent Lingiari at Daguragu, Northern Territory. His gesture symbolized the transfer of lands to the Gurindji people. Whitlam's government purchased an area of 3,236 square kilometers (1,250 square miles) from Wave Hill Station and gave it back to the Gurindji.

◀ Warren Snowdon (1950-), representing the district of Lingiari, tells the story of the Gurindji strike in his first speech as a member of Australia's Parliament. Lord Vestey (1941-) is the British nobleman who owned the cattle stations. Vincent Lingiari was the leader of the strike. Vestey tried to lure the strikers back to work by offering higher wages, but they held out for the recovery of their land.

4

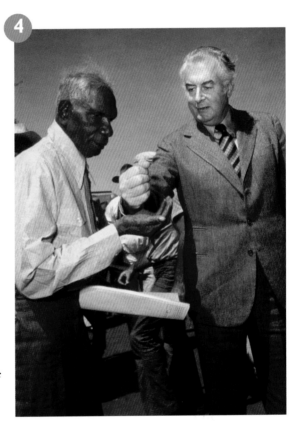

NOW YOU KNOW

- In 1966, Gurindji cattle workers in the Northern Territory went on strike and walked out.
- From their base at Wattie Creek, the strikers demanded payment for the land they had lost under white rule.
- In 1975, the Australian government returned a part of their land to the Gurindji people.

Land Rights: Paving the Way

IN THE LATE 1960'S, MANY ABORIGINES GREW DISCONTENTED at the slow pace of change. Some Aboriginal rights groups adopted more aggressive tactics, including the National Tribal Council (NTC), which did not accept white members. In 1972, rights leaders set up a tent "embassy" in the Australian capital of Canberra to protest the government's denial of land rights and lack of action. In the 1970's, however, government policies began to change. The Racial Discrimination Act of 1975 made it harder for states to discriminate against Aborigines.

▶ In 1971, representatives of the Yolngu people addressed this statement to Prime Minister William McMahon (1908-1988) after losing a court case over ownership of their ancestral lands. The dispute began in 1963. The Yolngu at Yirrkala Mission in the Northern Territory protested to the federal Parliament because the Australian government had given a mining company the right to operate on their lands. In such cases, Australian property law still denied the Aborigines any say.

1

The people of Yirrkala . . . are deeply shocked at the result of the recent Court case. We cannot be satisfied with anything less than ownership of the land. . . . The Australian law has said that the land is not ours. This is not so. It might be right legally but morally it's wrong. The law must be changed. The place does not belong to white man. They only want it for the money they can make. They will destroy plants, animal life and the culture of the people.

Raymattja Marika, Daymbalipu Mununggurr, and Wali Wunungmurra, 1971

2

◀ Protesters form a line to try to hold back police who intend to remove the Aboriginal Tent Embassy, on July 20, 1972. The Tent Embassy had been set up in January 1972 on the lawn of Parliament House in Canberra. The Embassy marked a new stage in Aboriginal protests; the use of "embassy" suggested that the Aborigines were a separate, independent nation, not part of Australia.

46

3

What I saw up there would put a shock into anyone. The police came running over in hundreds ... and began beating up on the Black women who had grabbed each other's hands and were standing in a big circle around the tent.... They punched them knocked them to the ground and then jumped on their guts. I couldn't believe my eyes. All this was taking place right outside Parliament House, that great white building where I was told the laws were made and the country is governed. The television cameras were everywhere but that didn't stop them.

Shirley Smith, 1981

◄ Shirley Smith (1921-1998), an Aboriginal rights leader of Wiradjuri descent, describes clashes with police at the Tent Embassy in her 1981 autobiography, *Mum Shirl.* The demonstrators refused police orders to leave, and the police tried to force them to go. People on both sides were injured.

▼ On Australia Day in January 1988, demonstrators protest the celebration of the 200th anniversary of white settlement. They carry an Australian Aboriginal flag, a yellow circle on a background of black and red, with slogans written on it.

4

NOW YOU KNOW

- In the late 1960's and the 1970's, the Yolngu failed to establish legal rights to their land.
- In 1972, demonstrators set up an Aboriginal Tent Embassy in Canberra to protest Australia's failure to compensate the Aborigines for the loss of their land.
- On the 200th anniversary of the settlement of Australia, Aboriginal rights leaders said the holiday should be called Invasion Day instead of Australia Day.

The Mabo Decision

THE MOVEMENT FOR LAND RIGHTS grew stronger in the 1990's. In 1992, after a 10-year legal battle, the High Court of Australia ruled in favor of Koiki Mabo (1936-1992) of Murray Island, one of the Torres Strait Islands. In the case of *Mabo v. Queensland*, the court ruled that Mabo's people had owned their land before the first British settlers arrived. The justices concluded that the theory of Australia as *terra nullius* (unoccupied land) was wrong. The Mabo case led to the Native Title Act of 1993, which upholds the traditional laws and customs of *indigenous* (original) peoples. The act allowed indigenous people to claim ownership of their traditional lands, if those lands were not already owned under Australian law.

1

Declare – (1) that the land in the Murray Islands is not Crown land within the meaning of that term . . . (2) that the Meriam people [the people of Murray Island, also called Mer] are entitled as against the whole world to possession, occupation, use and enjoyment of the island of Mer. . . .

High Court of Australia, 1992

◀ In June 1992, the High Court of Australia ruled that the Murray Islanders have successfully proved that their island, which they call Mer, has always belonged to them. The ruling meant that indigenous people could claim traditional lands that had previously been regarded as the property of the Crown (the Australian state).

2

▶ Koiki Mabo was a bold campaigner for land rights. He organized his people to take to court their claim to their ancestral land. Mabo died on Jan. 21, 1992, five months before the islanders won their historic victory in the High Court.

48

3

The great contemporary Aboriginal milestones of land rights and native title had effectively established Aborigines in the *bush* [remote areas] as the "real Aborigines" while *urban* [city] blacks remained ignored, impoverished and culturally isolated, an Aboriginal activist claimed yesterday.... Ms [Jacqui] Katona, the conference *convener* [organizer], said there was an overwhelming concern among delegates that land rights and the recognition of native title had left them out of the *equation* [consideration].

The Australian, 1994

▲ An article in *The Australian,* a national newspaper, reports on the Going Home Conference in October 1994 at Darwin in the Northern Territory. Human rights lawyers and campaigners for Aboriginal rights, including Jacqui Katona (1967?-) of the Djok people, organized the conference. It brought together hundreds of Aborigines who had been separated from their people. Many had descended from the kidnapped children of the "stolen generations" and had never learned about the traditions of their people. Others had lost touch with Aboriginal culture after moving to cities.

4

▲ Gladys Tybingoompa (1946-2006), a teacher of the Wik people, dances outside the High Court of Australia in Canberra in December 1996 to celebrate a victory for her people. The Wik claimed title over an area of leased ranch land in Queensland. The High Court ruled that ranchers and Aborigines could both have rights on the same land. Aborigines could use the land for traditional ceremonies and gatherings.

NOW YOU KNOW

- In 1992, the Murray Islanders won a High Court case that established their ownership of their homeland.

- In 1993, a new law, the Native Title Act, set up a system for carrying out the High Court ruling and restoring some lands to their traditional owners.

- In another important case, the High Court ruled in 1996 that Aboriginal people could have rights even on land that ranches had leased.

Bringing Them Home

In 1997, THE AUSTRALIAN HUMAN RIGHTS AND EQUAL OPPORTUNITY COMMISSION (now the Australian Human Rights Commission), a federal agency, released a report about the policy of removing children from Aboriginal families by force. The report, called *Bringing Them Home,* concluded that up to 100,000 children, called the stolen generations, had been taken in this way. It included heartbreaking accounts from the victims. After the report, there was a growing recognition that Australia had ignored Aboriginal rights.

1

[The white officials] grabbed us and put us in the back of a truck. As the truck left Phillip Creek everyone was crying and screaming. I remember mothers beating their heads with sticks and rocks. They were bleeding. They threw dirt over themselves. We were all crying in the truck, too. I remember seeing the mothers chasing the truck screaming and crying. And then they disappeared in the dust of the truck.

Lorna Cubillo, 1999

◀ In 1999, Lorna Cubillo explains in court how the authorities took her and 16 other children from their homes. Cubillo was taken from Phillip Creek, Northern Territory, in 1947, when she was 7 or 8 years old. She sued the Australian government in the Federal Court of Australia for *compensation* (payment) for her suffering, but the judge dismissed her case.

▼ The 2002 film *Rabbit-Proof Fence* tells the true story of three Aboriginal girls who were taken from their homes but escaped. They returned home by following a pest-control fence for 1,500 miles (2,400 kilometers). The film is based on the 1996 book *Follow the Rabbit-Proof Fence* by Doris Pilkington, the daughter of one of the girls.

2

50

3

> The policy of forcible removal of children from Indigenous Australians to other groups for the purpose of raising them separately from and ignorant of their culture and people could properly be labelled "genocidal" in breach of binding international law from at least 11 December 1946. . . . The practice continued for almost another quarter of a century.
>
> *Bringing Them Home*, 1997

▲ The *Bringing Them Home* report calls the government policy of removing children from Aboriginal families a form of *genocide* (extermination of an entire people). The Australian Human Rights and Equal Opportunity Commission produced the report. Its references to genocide caused controversy amongst scholars, politicians, and the public.

4

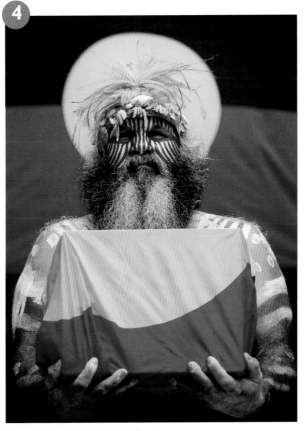

▲ On July 29, 2003, Major Sumner (1948?-   ), an elder of the Ngarrindjeri people, receives from the University of Manchester a box containing the skulls of four Aborigines, for return to Australia. In the past, British scientists took many Aboriginal remains to study them. According to traditional Aboriginal beliefs, the dead cannot enter the spirit world until their remains are laid to rest.

NOW YOU KNOW

- During the 1990's, many Australians began to recognize that their country had ignored Aboriginal rights.
- In 1997, the government's *Bringing Them Home* report criticized the policy of removing Aboriginal children from their homes.
- The report said that the removal of children was genocidal because it aimed to wipe out the Aboriginal people and their culture.

Reconciliation Begins

I N 1991, THE AUSTRALIAN PARLIAMENT ESTABLISHED THE COUNCIL FOR ABORIGINAL RECONCILIATION. Its aim was to achieve *reconciliation* between Aborigines and non-Aborigines—that is, bringing the two communities together in friendship. The council hoped to reach its goal by 2001, the 100th anniversary of Australian federation. The first decade of reconciliation was celebrated at an event called Corroboree 2000. But Aboriginal rights protests continued. Life in Aboriginal communities showed little improvement. Aborigines remained the most disadvantaged group in Australia. They had the lowest incomes, the worst housing, the least education, the shortest life expectancy, and the highest chance of being arrested and imprisoned.

1

Reconciliation will not work if it puts a higher value on symbolic gestures and overblown promises rather than practical needs of Aboriginal and Torres Strait Islander people in areas like health, housing, education and employment. It will not work if it is premised [based] solely on a sense of national guilt and shame. Rather we should acknowledge past injustices and focus our energies on addressing the root causes of current and future disadvantage among our indigenous people

Prime Minister John Winston Howard, 1997

◀ In a speech to the Australian Reconciliation Convention in Melbourne, Victoria, in May 1997, Prime Minister John W. Howard (1939-   ) refused to apologize to indigenous people for their past mistreatment. He argues that the Aborigines have greater need of practical measures to improve their lives. Most Aboriginal leaders saw an apology from the prime minister as a vital part of the healing process. The Council for Aboriginal Reconciliation held the three-day convention at which Aborigines and non-Aborigines discussed issues related to reconciliation.

2

Now it's turned very nasty, ugly. It is now going to be violent and we're telling all the British people, "Please, don't come over. If you want to see burning cars and burning buildings then come over. Enjoy yourself. But if you want to come to the [2000 Summer Olympic] Games, come to the Games and go straight home again."

Charles Perkins, 2000

▶ The Aboriginal rights leader Charles Perkins, who led the first Freedom Ride in 1965, warns in a radio interview of likely violence at the 2000 Sydney Olympic Games. Although no violence occurred, Perkins's comments reflected the anger felt by many Aborigines at the time. Howard's refusal to apologize for their past mistreatment had strained relations between the government and the Aboriginal community. Things got worse during 2000. The government claimed that there had been no stolen generations, that only 10 percent of Aboriginal families had been affected, and that many of the children had been removed for their own good.

52

▼ More than 200,000 people march across Sydney Harbour Bridge on May 28, 2000, in support of Aboriginal rights during an event called Corroboree 2000. *Corroboree* is an Aboriginal word meaning *gathering*. The marchers carry the Aboriginal flag, which was designed in 1971. The black bar on the flag represents Australia's indigenous people. The red one symbolizes the earth. The yellow circle stands for the sun.

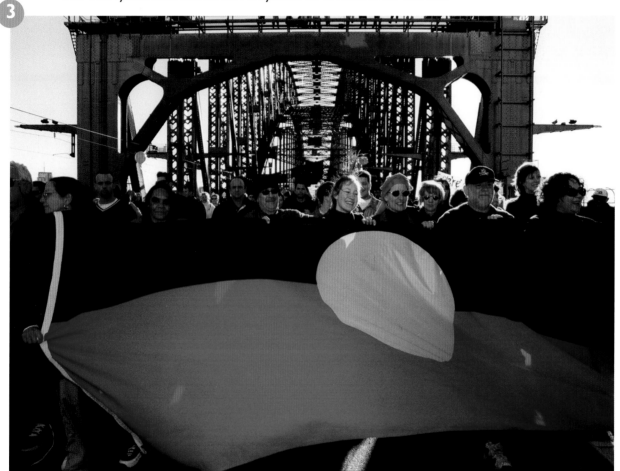

NOW YOU KNOW

- A Council for Aboriginal Reconciliation operated from 1991 to 2001.
- Prime Minister John Howard refused to apologize to the Aborigines, arguing that it was more meaningful to deal with their practical difficulties.
- Many Aborigines were frustrated by the lack of an apology or any real improvements in their lives, and they continued to protest.

Saying Sorry

IN 2007, AUSTRALIAN VOTERS ELECTED A NEW GOVERNMENT, and Kevin Rudd (1957-) became prime minister. Unlike John Howard, Rudd believed that an official apology would play an essential part in reconciling Aborigines and non-Aborigines. On Feb. 13, 2008, Rudd made a speech of apology. He stated that the government and people of Australia were sorry for the past mistreatment of indigenous people in general and for the stolen generations in particular. Rudd committed his government to "closing the gap" between the living standards of indigenous people and other Australians. He promised to give a yearly progress report.

▶ In a speech to Parliament in February 2008, Prime Minister Kevin Rudd apologizes to Australia's indigenous peoples for past mistreatment. The 1997 report *Bringing Them Home* had recommended such an apology. The report also advised paying compensation to Aborigines who had suffered under the child-removal policy, but Rudd's government did not commit itself to making such payments.

▼ An Aboriginal family listens outside Parliament House in Canberra to Kevin Rudd's apology. They hold pictures of loved ones who have died.

1

The time has now come for the nation to turn a new page in Australia's history by righting the wrongs of the past and so moving forward with confidence to the future. We apologise for the laws and policies of successive Parliaments and governments that have inflicted profound grief, suffering and loss on these our fellow Australians. We apologise especially for the removal of Aboriginal and Torres Strait Islander children from their families, their communities and their country. For the pain, suffering and hurt of these Stolen Generations, their descendants and for their families left behind, we say sorry.

Kevin Rudd, 2008

2

54

3

◀ Prime Minister Kevin Rudd hugs an Aboriginal woman after delivering his apology speech. Large crowds of people gathered in public places throughout Australia to watch the apology televised on big screens. Some people wept.

▶ Noel Pearson (1965-), a lawyer and Aboriginal rights leader, expresses doubts about Prime Minister Rudd's apology in a 2009 collection of writings titled *Up from the Mission*. Pearson fears that Australia would use the apology to "move on," forget about past mistreatment of Aborigines, and take little or no further action. Most rights campaigners welcomed the apology, but they wanted action to improve opportunities for indigenous people.

4

There is no doubt that the majority of political leaders and ordinary white Australians hope that the country will be able to, to use the prime minister's own words, "move on." There are two ways to interpret this hope. The first is *ominous* [threatening]: that it represents a hope to dispose of the apology in as decent (and politically and financially costless) a way as possible, and to put the whole subject into the "that box is ticked" [checked off] category. The second is *optimistic* [hopeful]: that it represents a necessary starting-point for a genuinely hopeful era in Indigenous affairs.

Noel Pearson, 2009

NOW YOU KNOW

- In 2008, Prime Minister Kevin Rudd issued an apology to Aborigines and in particular to the stolen generations.
- Rudd committed to a program of "closing the gap" between the disadvantaged indigenous peoples and other Australians.
- Most Aborigines welcomed the apology and hoped Rudd would take action to end inequality.

We Have Survived

IN 2010, THERE WERE MORE THAN 500,000 ABORIGINES AND Torres Strait Islanders in Australia, making up 2.5 percent of the population. Despite the harmful actions of governments, officials, and others from 1788 to the 1970's, Aboriginal culture and identity have survived. The people have passed down songs and dances through the generations. Rock paintings document thousands of years of their history. Today, Aboriginal artists and musicians work in both traditional and nontraditional styles. Aborigines have been elected to political office and have become successful athletes, doctors, lawyers, and writers.

▶ Tom Calma (1953-), a former commissioner on the Australian Human Rights Commission, draws attention to the achievements of the Aboriginal people and the survival of their culture. Calma, who is of Kungarakan and Iwaidja ancestry, spoke in Victoria Park in Sydney on Jan. 26, 2010— Australia Day to most Australians. However, many Aborigines prefer to call it "Survival Day."

... we as Aboriginal and Torres Strait Islander peoples come together on what has been named "Australia Day" to celebrate our resilience [ability to recover] and our survival. We call it Survival Day. On this day we reflect on the struggle and the success of our elders; those who have come before us; and many of whom are still with us and continue the fight; who have ensured a legacy of opportunity for our people.
Tom Calma, 2010

◀ The Aboriginal musicians Archie Roach (1956-) and Ruby Hunter (1955-2010) perform in 2001. Both belonged to the stolen generations. Officials removed them from their families when they were young children. They grew up in institutions and foster care and met when they both were homeless teenagers. Roach and Hunter married and had five children. They performed together until Hunter's death in February 2010.

56

3

...as a community, we should be more willing to celebrate and learn from our successes. I believe, that despite the gloom of the present, we have every reason to be optimistic in recognising the presence of an emerging class of young Indigenous leaders to open a new phase in defining black/white relations. 410,000 [the Aborigine population at that time] is not a lot of people. We can turn our future around.

Aden Ridgeway, 2002

◀ Aden Ridgeway (1962-), a political leader of the Gumbayyngirr people, expresses his optimistic vision of the future in a 2002 speech in Sydney. Ridgeway, a Democrat, represented New South Wales in the Australian Senate from 1999 to 2005. He was only the second Aboriginal member of Parliament, after Neville Bonner (1922-1999), who served from 1971 to 1983. Today, a number of Aborigines have successful political careers.

4

◀ Faith Butler Nungarayi (1950-), an artist of the Ngaanyatjarra people, stands before one of her paintings during a 2008 exhibition in Melbourne. The work, *Tjalili*, includes traditional designs that were formerly used in rock art or as body decoration. Blending traditional and modern ideas is typical of present-day Aboriginal art.

NOW YOU KNOW

- Today, Aborigines and Torres Strait Islanders make up about 2.5 percent of the population of Australia.
- Indigenous people have achieved successes in the arts, politics, and other professions.
- Many Aborigines celebrate Australia Day as "Survival Day."

The Struggle Continues

THE FEDERAL AND STATE GOVERNMENTS HAVE PROMISED to tackle the disadvantages faced by indigenous people. Much remains to be done. Many Aboriginal people still suffer from bad health and substandard housing and sanitation. Poor education, high unemployment, and low pay remain problems. Although indigenous people make up less than 3 percent of the population, they are a quarter of the prison population. In 2008, Prime Minister Kevin Rudd promised new investment to help. But his yearly report in February 2010 admitted that "progress is clearly too slow."

▶ Michael J. (Mick) Dodson, a lawyer and government official of the Yawuru people, draws attention to the real suffering that lies behind health statistics. Dodson's 1994 report for the Aboriginal and Torres Strait Islander Social Justice Commission revealed that indigenous people suffer more from disease, die younger, and lose more children in infancy than white Australians.

❶ The meaning of these figures is not heard—or felt. The statistics of infant and *perinatal mortality* [deaths of infants and small children] are our babies and children who die in our arms. . . . The statistics of shortened life expectancy are our mothers and fathers, uncles, aunties and elders who live diminished lives and die before their gifts of knowledge and experience are passed on. We die silently under these statistics.

Michael J. Dodson, 1994

❷ ◀ Children play in 2001 among "The Sea of Hands," a large public art installation organized by Australians for Native Title and Reconciliation (ANTaR). ANTaR is a group of mostly non-Aboriginal people and organizations that supports the rights of Aborigines to maintain their culture. It put up these plastic hands in Australia's large cities for the public to sign as a way of showing their support for Aboriginal rights. Hundreds of thousands of Australians have signed their names.

3

I'm not racist but...
They're all drunks?
They don't wash?
The kids roam the streets at night?
They look dangerous!!!

I'm not racist but...
I wouldn't pick one up in my cab
I wouldn't want my daughter to
 marry one
I wouldn't rent my flat to one
I wouldn't employ one

Anita Heiss,
"I'm Not Racist But," 2008

◀ A poem by Aboriginal writer Anita Heiss (1968-   ) of the Wiradjuri people highlights some common attitudes toward indigenous people. It suggests that many people who think they are not racist actually have many racist ideas about Aboriginal people.

4

▶ Combining the traditional with the modern, an Aborigine displays body paint while holding a digital camera. Aboriginal and human rights activists continue to campaign to help indigenous people maintain their traditions while also benefiting from modern technology, education, housing, and health care.

NOW YOU KNOW

- The Australian government has promised to improve Aboriginal people's living standards and opportunities.
- In February 2010, Prime Minister Kevin Rudd admitted that progress in improving life for Aborigines was still too slow.
- Aboriginal and human rights groups continue to campaign to help indigenous people preserve their culture and traditions.

Timeline

c.50,000 B.C.	Aborigines arrive in Australia from Southeast Asia.
A.D. 1606	Willem Jansz, a Dutch sea captain, sails to Australia.
1770	Captain James Cook claims the east coast of Australia for Britain (now part of the United Kingdom) and names it New South Wales.
1788	The First Fleet arrives from Britain and sets up a penal colony at Port Jackson (later Sydney).
1803	The British establish a penal colony on the island of Tasmania, south of mainland Australia.
1829-1834	Truganini and George Augustus Robinson lead the Tasmanian Aborigines to Flinders Island.
1863	The Aborigines of Victoria establish a reserve called Coranderrk Aboriginal Station.
1869	The colony of Victoria passes the first Aboriginal Protection Act.
1881	New South Wales sets up the Cummeragunja Mission.
1886	In Victoria, removal of mixed-race children from Aboriginal reserves begins.
1901	The six Australian colonies become states within the Commonwealth of Australia.
1909	The Aborigines Protection Act of New South Wales gives the Aborigines Protection Board the right to remove Aboriginal children from their families.
1925	Aboriginal and white leaders found the Australian Aboriginal Progressive Association (AAPA), one of the first Aboriginal rights organizations.
1936	The Australian Aborigines' League (AAL) is founded.
1938	Aborigines protest the 150th anniversary of white settlement, declaring it a Day of Mourning.
1939	Aborigines leave the Cummeragunja Mission to protest against the conditions there and the removal of their children.
1940's	State governments begin to issue exemption certificates granting citizenship rights to Aborigines willing to adopt a white lifestyle and values.
1946	In the Pilbara region of Western Australia, Aboriginal *stockmen* (ranch workers) go on strike until, in 1949, they win better pay.
1958	The first national organization for Aborigines, the Federal Council for Aboriginal Advancement (FCAA), is founded.
1964	The FCAA is renamed the Federal Council for the Advancement of Aborigines and Torres Strait Islanders (FCAATSI).
1965	Charles Perkins, an Aboriginal university student, leads a Freedom Ride to publicize segregation and discrimination across Australia.
1966	Gurindji people in the Northern Territory go on strike to protest their conditions and set up a new community at Wattie Creek. The strike ends when they win some of their demands in 1975.
1967	Australians vote in favor of giving Aborigines citizenship rights.
1971	The Yolngu people lose a court case over ownership of their ancestral lands.
1972	Aborigine leaders set up an Aboriginal Tent Embassy outside Parliament House.
1975	The Racial Discrimination Act becomes law.
1991	Parliament sets up the Council for Aboriginal Reconciliation. It operates until 2001.
1992	The Murray Islanders win the land rights case started by Koiki Mabo.
1993	The Native Title Act makes it possible for *indigenous* (original) people to claim ownership of their lands.
1996	The Wik people win their land rights case.
1997	A federal government agency publishes the *Bringing Them Home* report. It sharply criticizes the forced removal of Aboriginal children from their families.
2000	During the Corroboree 2000 reconciliation event, more than 200,000 people take part in a walk over Sydney Harbour Bridge in support of reconciliation.
2008	Prime Minister Kevin Rudd apologizes to indigenous Australians and to the stolen generations.

Sources

4-5 Document 1 – Patten, J. T., and W. Ferguson, *Aborigines Claim Citizen Rights!* Sydney: Publicist, 1938. Print. In *The Struggle for Aboriginal Rights: A Documentary History.* Comp. Bain Attwood and Andrew Markus. St. Leonards: Allen & Unwin, 1999. Print. Document 3 – Bowler, Jim. "John Mulvaney: An Amazing Journey." *The University of Melbourne News.* Univ. of Melbourne, 16 May 2005. Web. 16 June 2010.

6-7 Document 1 – Neidjie, Bill, Stephen Davis, and Allan Fox. *Australia's Kakadu Man.* Darwin: Resource Managers, 1986. Print. Document 2 – Lester, Yami. *Yami: The Autobiography of Yami Lester.* 2nd ed. Alice Springs, Australia: Jukurrpa Books, 2000. Print.

8-9 Document 1 – Cook, James. "Cook's Journal: Daily Entries: 22 August 1770." *Cook's Endeavour Journal.* Web. 16 June 2010. Document 3 – Bradley, William. Journal Titled 'A Voyage to New South Wales,' December 1786-May 1792; Compiled 1802+." *State Library of New South Wales.* Web. 21 June 2010.

10-11 Document 1 – Tench, Watkin. *A Complete Account of the Settlement at Port Jackson.* 1793. Teddington, Middlesex: Echo Library, 2006. Print. Document 3 – Bennelong. Letter to Mr. Phillips. 29 Aug. 1796. In *Telling Stories: Indigenous History and Memory in Australia and New Zealand.* Ed. Bain Attwood and Fiona Magowan. Crows Nest, NSW: Allen & Unwin, 2001. Print.

12-13 Document 1 – Collins, David. *An Account of the English Colony in New South Wales,* 1798. Teddington, Middlesex: Echo Library, 2008. Print. Document 2 – Threlkeld, Lancelot E. Memorandum of public meeting at Bathurst, 1824. In *Australian Reminiscences & Papers of L. E. Threlkeld, Missionary to the Aborigines, 1824-1859.* Ed. Niel Gunson, Canberra: Australian Institute of Aboriginal Studies, 1974. Print.

14-15 Document 1 – Editorial. *Colonial Times and Tasmanian Advertiser* [Hobart, Tas.] 1 Dec. 1826: 2-3. *Australian Newspapers(1803-1854).* Web. 16 June 2010. Document 3 – Tasmanian Aborigines of Flinders Island. Petition to Queen Victoria. 17 Feb. 1846. In *The Struggle for Aboriginal Rights: A Documentary History.* Comp. Bain Attwood and Andrew Markus. St. Leonards: Allen & Unwin, 1999. Print.

16-17 Document 1 – Colony of Victoria. Aboriginal Protection Act 1869. 11 Nov. 1869. *National Archives of Australia – Documenting a Democracy.* Web. 16 June 2010. Document 3 – Article in *The Age* [Melbourne newspaper]. 11 Jan 1888. Quoted in *Dispossession: Black Australians and White Invaders.* Comp. Henry Reynolds. Sydney: Allen & Unwin, 1989. Print.

18-19 Document 1 – Marks, Ivy. Interview by Genevieve Grieves. 2003. *Voices of Lake Tyers.* Australian Broadcasting Corporation, 2004. Web. 16 June 2010. Document 3 – Poonindie Petition. 2 Feb. 1894. In *The Struggle for Aboriginal Rights: A Documentary History.* Comp. Bain Attwood and Andrew Markus. St. Leonards: Allen & Unwin, 1999. Print.

20-21 Document 1 – "Point Macleay Natives Want More Food and Less Prayer." *Advertiser* [Adelaide, SA] 12 April 1907: 4. *Australian Newspapers(1803-1854).* Web. 16 June 2010. Document 2 – Matthews, Daniel, "Native Tribes of the Upper Murray." 11 Aug. 1899. In *Proceedings of the Royal Geographical Society of Australasia: South Australian Branch.* Vol. 4. Adelaide, SA: W. K. Thomas & Co., 1901. *Google Books.* Web. 16 June 2010.

22-23 Document 1 – Bamfield, Thomas. Letter to the Board Appointed to Inquire into Coranderrk Aboriginal Station. 30 Sept. 1881. In *The Struggle for Aboriginal Rights: A Documentary History.* Comp. Bain Attwood and Andrew Markus. St. Leonards: Allen & Unwin, 1999. Print. Document 3 – Aborigines of Coranderrk. Petition to the Chief Secretary of Victoria. 21 Sept. 1886. In *The Struggle for Aboriginal Rights: A Documentary History.* Comp. Bain Attwood and Andrew Markus. St. Leonards: Allen & Unwin, 1999. Print.

24-25 Document 2 – Commonwealth of Australia Constitution Act 1900. 9 July 1900. *National Archives of Australia – Documenting a Democracy.* Web. 16 June 2010. Document 3 – "The Western Australian Aborigines." *Sydney Morning Herald,* 1 Feb. 1905: 6. *Australian Newspapers(1803-1854).* Web. 16 June 2010.

26-27 Document 1 – New South Wales. Aborigines Protection Act 1909. 20 Dec. 1909. *AIATSIS.gov.* Web. 16 June 2010. Document 3 – Neville, A. O. Statement to the Conference of Commonwealth and State Aboriginal Authorities. 21 April 1937. In *Genocide and Settler Society.* Ed. A. Dirk Moses. New York: Berghahn Books, 2004. Print.

28-29 Document 1 – Hatton, Elizabeth McKenzie. Letter to the editor of *The Voice of the North* [New South Wales newspaper]. 12 June 1925. In *The Struggle for Aboriginal Rights: A Documentary History.* In *The Struggle for Aboriginal Rights: A Documentary History.* Comp. Bain Attwood and Andrew Markus. St. Leonards: Allen & Unwin, 1999. Print. Document 2 – Cooper, William. Petition to the King. 1934. *National Archives of Australia – Documenting a Democracy.* Web. 16 June 2010.

30-31 Document 1 – Patten, Jack. Speech at the Day of Mourning and Protest. 26 Jan. 1938. In "Our Historic Day of Mourning & Protest." *Australian Abo Call* [Aboriginal newspaper] April 1938: 2. *AIATSIS.gov.* Web. 16 June 2010. Document 4 – Aboriginal Deputation to Prime Minister Joseph Lyons. 31 Jan.

1938. In "Deputation to the Prime Minister." *Australian Abo Call* [Aboriginal newspaper] April 1938: 1. *State Library New South Wales.* Web. 16 June 2010.

32-33 Document 1 – Tucker, Margaret. Letter to *Worker's Voice* [communist Party newspaper]. 1 March 1939. In *The Struggle for Aboriginal Rights: A Documentary History.* Comp. Bain Attwood and Andrew Markus. St. Leonards: Allen & Unwin, 1999. Print. Document 2 – "N.S.W. Mission Station Man Convicted." *Argus* [Melbourne], 11 March 1939:2. *Australian Newspapers(1803-1854).* Web. 16 June 2010.

34-35 Document 1 – Gibbs, Pearl. Radio broadcast. 8 June 1941. In *The Struggle for Aboriginal Rights: A Documentary History.* Comp. Bain Attwood and Andrew Markus. St. Leonards: Allen & Unwin, 1999. Print.

36-37 Document 1 – Pickwick, Beulah. Interview recorded for the exhibition "From Little Things Big Things Grow" (10 Sept. 2009 to 8 March 2010). *National Museum of Australia, Canberra.* Web. 25 May 2010. Document 2 – New South Wales. Aborigines Protection Act 1909-1943, Sect. 18c (Regulation 56). *Discovering Democracy.* Web. 18 June 2010.

38-39 Document 1 – Groves, Bert. Speech to the Federal Council for Aboriginal Advancement. February 1958. In Lake, Marilyn. *Faith: Faith Bender, Gentle Activist.* St. Leonards: Allen & Unwin, 2002. Print. Document 3 – McGinness, Joe. Speech for the Campaign to Save Lake Tyers. 22 May 1963. In *The Struggle for Aboriginal Rights: A Documentary History.* Comp. Bain Attwood and Andrew Markus. St. Leonards: Allen & Unwin, 1999. Print.

40-41 Document 1 – Sydney University Organising Committee for Action on Aboriginal Rights. Leaflet advertising a meeting on 7 July 1964. In Curthoys, Ann. *Freedom Ride: A Freedom Rider Remembers.* Crows Nest, NSW: Allen & Unwin, 2002. Print. Document 3 – Stone, Gerry. "Violence Explodes in Racist Town: Moree Battles Students." *Sunday Mirror* [Sydney]. 21 Feb. 1965. *Collaborating for Indigenous Rights.* Web. 18 June 2010.

42-43 Document 1 – Andrews, Shirley. Letter announcing the launch of a petition to amend Australia's Constitution, 1962. In Attwood, Bain, and Andrew Markus. *The 1967 Referendum: Race, Power and the Australian Constitution.* 2nd ed. Canberra: Aboriginal Studies Press, 2007. Print. Document 3 – Onus, Bill. Interview in *The Age* [Melbourne newspaper]. 11 April 1967. In Attwood, Bain, and Andrew Markus. *The 1967 Referendum: Race, Power and the Australian Constitution.* 2nd ed. Canberra: Aboriginal Studies Press, 2007.

44-45 Document 1 – Bernard, Ida. "An Oral History from the Wave Hill Strike." *Green Left Weekly* 23 Oct. 1996. n pag. *Green Left Weekly.* Web. 26 May 2010. Document 3 – Snowdon, Warren. Speech to Parliament. 20 March 2002. *The Hon. Warren Snowdon MP.* Web. 15 June 2010.

46-47 Document 1 – Marika, Raymattja, Daymbalipu Mununggurr, and Wali Wunungmurra. Statement to Prime Minister William McMahon. 6 May 1971. In *The Struggle for Aboriginal Rights: A Documentary History.* Comp. Bain Attwood and Andrew Markus. St. Leonards: Allen & Unwin, 1999. Print. Document 3 – Smith, Shirley. *Mum Shirl: An Autobiography.* Melbourne: Heinemann, 1981. Print.

48-49 Document 1 – Mabo and Others v. Queensland [No. 2]. High Court of Australia. 1992. *National Archives of Australia – Documenting a Democracy.* Web. 21 June 2010. Document 3 – Article in *The Australian* [newspaper]. 6 Oct. 1994. In *The Struggle for Aboriginal Rights: A Documentary History.* Comp. Bain Attwood and Andrew Markus. St. Leonards: Allen & Unwin, 1999. Print.

50-51 Document 1 – Cubillo, Lorna. Testimony in Gunner and Cubillo v. the Commonwealth. 1999. In Knightley, Phillip. *Australia: A Biography of a Nation.* London: Jonathan Cape, 2000. Print. Document 3 – Australia. Human Rights and Equal Opportunity Commission. *Bringing Them Home.* Sydney: Human Rights and Equal Opportunity Commission, 1997. *Australian Human Rights Commission.* Web. 21 June 2010.

52-53 Document 1 – Howard, John Winston. Speech to the Australian Reconciliation Convention. May 1997. *Indigenous Law Resources.* Web. 21 June 2010. Document 2 – Perkins, Charles. Interview by a BBC reporter. 2 April 2000. *AM* [Australian Broadcasting Corporation]. Web. 27 May 2010.

54-55 Document 1 – Rudd, Kevin. "Apology to Australia's Indigenous Peoples." Speech to the House of Representatives. 13 Feb. 2008. In King, Jonathan. *Great Moments in Australian History.* Crows Nest: Allen & Unwin, 2009. Print. Document 4 – Pearson, Noel. *Up from the Mission: Selected Writings.* Melbourne: Black Inc., 2009. Print.

56-57 Document 1 – Calma, Tom. "Looking Back, Looking Forward." Kevin Cook Lecture. 26 Jan. 2010. *Australian Human Rights Commission.* Web. 21 June 2010. Document 3 – Ridgeway, Aden. "Sydney Launch of Social Justice Report, 2001." 17 July 2002. *Australian Human Rights Commission.* Web. 21 June 2010.

58-59 Document 1 – Aboriginal and Torres Strait Islander Social Justice Commission. *Second Report 1994.* Canberra: AGPS, 1994. *Indigenous Law Resources.* Web. 21 June 2010. Document 3 – Heiss, Anita. "I'm Not Racist But." In *I'm Not Racist, But...: A Collection of Social Observations.* Cambridge: Salt Publishing, 2008. Print.

Additional resources

Books

Aboriginal Art & Culture, by Jane Bingham, Raintree, 2005

Aboriginal Australians (Indigenous Peoples series), by Diana Marshall, Weigl Publishers, 2003

The Aboriginal People of Australia (First Peoples series) by Anne Bartlett, Lerner, 2001

Australian Aborigines (Early Peoples series), World Book, Inc., 2009

First Australians: An Illustrated History, by Rachel Perkins and Marcia Langton, Miegunyah Press, 2008

Websites

http://www.abc.net.au/indigenous/
An Australian Broadcasting Corporation (ABC) site showcases the achievements of Aborigines and Torres Strait Islanders.

http://www.abc.net.au/schoolstv/nations/
The ABC's "Many Nations, One People" site provides information about Aboriginal society and culture.

http://www1.aiatsis.gov.au
The website of the Australian Institute of Aboriginal and Torres Strait Islander Studies has information about the cultures and lifestyles of Aboriginal and Torres Strait Islander peoples.

http://indigenousrights.net.au/
The National Museum of Australia's website "Collaborating for Indigenous Rights" has historical documents from the period 1957 to 1973.

http://www.indigenousaustralia.info
The "Indigenous Australia" site has information on Aboriginal art, culture, and history.

http://www.humanrights.gov.au/Social_Justice/bth_report/report/ch17.html
The Australian Human Rights Commission website deals with social justice issues relating to Aborigines and Torres Strait Islanders.

Index

Index

Acknowledgments

AKG-Images: 12; **Australian Human Rights Commission:** 26 ('Between Two Worlds' Australian Archives); **Australian War Memorial:** 36 (Donor S. Clark); **Bridgeman Art Library:** 14 (National Library of Australia), 45 (Hallmark Cards Australian Photography Collection Fund 1991); **Corbis:** 4 (Penny Tweedie), 6 (Dave Jacobs/Monsoon/Photolibrary), 9 (Christel Gerstenberg), 18 (Cannon Collection/Australian Picture Library), 44 (Bettmann), 47 (Penny Tweedie), 51 (Reuters/Ian Hodgson), 55 (Ramage Gary/Pool/Reuters), 56 (John Van Hasselt/Sygma), 57 (Mick Tsikas/Reuters), 58 (John Van Hasselt/Sygma); **FCAATSI:** 42; **Getty:** 8 (Time & Life Pictures), 17 (Popperfoto), 19 (Popperfoto), 24 (Hulton Archive); **Kobal Collection:** 50 (Miramax/Dimension Films/Penny Tweedie); **Mary Evans Picture Library:** 23; **National Library of Australia:** 22, 29 ; **National Museum of Australia:** 41 (Courtesy of the Herald & Weekly Times Pty Ltd); **Northern Territory Library:** 35 (PH0323/0012,D. D. Smith); **Office of the Chief Parliamentary Counsel:** 16 (Extract reproduced with the permission of the Crown in the right of the State of Victoria, Australia); **Photoshot:** 30, 38 (R L Stewart/Picture Media), 1, 39 (The Age Archive/Picture Media), 43 (George Lipman/Picture Media), 46 (Picture Media), 48 (Jim McEwan/Picture Media), 53 (Rick Stevens/Picture Media), 54 (Justin McManus/Picture Media); **Rex Features:** 5, 40, 49; **Scholars' Centre, University of Western Australia Library:** 27; **State Library of New South Wales:** 11; **State Library of Victoria:** 20 (Charles Walter, La Trobe Picture Collection); **Tasmanian Museum and Art Gallery:** 15; **TopFoto:** 10 (Ullstein Bild), 59 (ImageWorks).

Cover main image: **Getty** (William West/AFP); inset image: **Photoshot** (The Age Archive/Picture Media)

Excerpt from "I'm Not a Racist But ..." Permission granted by Salt Publishing, © Anita Heiss.